faith
undiluted

connie-anne barrett

AMBASSADOR INTERNATIONAL
Greenville, South Carolina • Belfast, Northern Ireland

FAITH UNDILUTED
© Copyright 2009 Connie-Anne Barrett

ISBN 978-1-84030-218-9

Ambassador Publications
a division of
Ambassador Productions Ltd.
Providence House
Ardenlee Street,
Belfast,
BT6 8QJ
Northern Ireland
www.ambassador-productions.com

Emerald House
427 Wade Hampton Blvd.
Greenville
SC 29609, USA
www.emeraldhouse.com

faith
undiluted

this title comes from the fact that all too often we water down
our faith until it's so weak and watery it's no use to anyone.
God definitely doesn't want us to dilute down our faith,
He doesn't want our standards to slip.

a thousand thank-yous

Laura Gordon- you've been a brick, a wee rock from the very start! God loved me so much He gave me you, and I love Him all the more for it :]

Rick Hill- I am eternally indebted for all your insight and input... thanks for coming alongside me and not only sharing the vision, but running with it.

Glenda Crawford- thanks for your energy and enthusiasm, you've been the best! Thanks for believing in me and giving me the final push. Much love...

Karen Strong- the fastest speed-reader of the west! I appreciate your ongoing support, your willingness to give a helping hand is a testimony to you.

Mark & Claire McClurg- just knowing that you two are behind me has meant so much. Thanks for all your words of wisdom Pastor and your encouragement Claire.

The Barrett Clan- thanks for the endless cups of tea and understanding (special thanks goes to Abigail, thank-you for your first-class secret-keeping)

I am forever thankful for you all, love and hugs... Connie :]

how to use this tool

The prime time to meet with God is before the world wakes up. Set your alarm clock and stick to it. Now I'm not saying you have to get up at the break of dawn, just do your devotions before you start the day. If you don't you could be in danger of getting distracted and end up squeezing God in at the end of the day. I'd also keep in mind that it's not the brightest idea to set a time on it or else you could end up limiting the Lord.

Here's the sad truth, we would sooner look to ourselves than to the Scriptures. This isn't right, this isn't the way it should be. Don't stunt your spiritual growth! **Fuel on His Word**, drink deep at the Fountain of living water.

Read through the Bible passages that I've highlighted, read and re-read them if need be. Always have your Bible at the ready when you're doing your devotions, God's Word carries far more weight that my words. And while you're at it, don't just read, **worship!**

Once you've read the prayer I've tagged on at the end please **pray on**. Don't just parrot my prayers, talk to God for yourself. Always remember that if you try and find time to pray something will always crop up. You have to set aside time to spend with God. We are meant to make a habit of it. We are meant to be disciples DAILY.

Don't rush through it, read them one at a time. Make good use of the exercises, fill in the spaces with your thoughts. Answer all the questions and **answer honestly**. It's always a good idea to keep a journal by your side as you do your devotions. If the space around the exercises isn't enough you can scribble away to your heart's content. When you do this I can promise you that your faith will go from strength to strength.

Please home in on the summaries, think upon these things day in and day out. Learn them off if you can, it makes it easier to live them out. Here's what the summaries stand for:

BIBLE BONES - foundations of faith, bits of the Bible that our faith is based on

THINK UPON THESE THINGS - something to chew on, something to mull over in your mind

POINT TO PONDER? - something for further thought, something to get your brain in gear

Above all I hope and pray that you work this into your routine and EXERCISE IT OUT! I pray that you wouldn't just learn to love His laws, but that you would **live them out** as well. I hope that His Word finds a home in your heart.

Bible Abbreviations

- Amplified Bible- Amplified
- Contemporary English Version- CEV
- Darby Translation
- English Standard Version- ESV
- New American Standard Bible- NASB
- New Century Version- NCV

- New International Version- NIV
- New International Version UK- NIV UK
- New King James Version- NKJV
- New Living Translation/Version- NLT
- The Message- MSG

contents

1   the power of prayer   9
2   God of the impossible   11
3   back to basics   13
4   perfect plan   15
5   don't just dream it, do it!   17
6   are we limiting the Lord?   19
7   stealing centre-stage   21
8   for the glory of God   23
9   the Light of Life   26
10   heavy heart   28
11   a God-hug   30
12   "the hall of nobodies"   32
13   the counterfeit christ
     uncovered   34
14   God's plan prevails   36

15   seek out to serve   38
16   fake Pharisees   41
17   ask in accordance   44
18   the Father's love   46
19   garbage gift-wrapped   49
20   crimes against Christ   52
21   free as free can be   54
22   miracle-worker   56
23   singled out for something
     special   59
24   God in disguise   61
25   living prayer   64
26   God-given gift   66
27   a devil in disguise   69
28   driving disaster   72

29 a bog-standard bunch 74
30 "pick 'n' mix Christians" 76
31 a glimpse of God 79
32 modern day hermit 82
33 geek for God! 85
34 chaos? 88
35 jumble-sale junk 91
36 the story of Teddy Edward 93
37 walk your talk 95
38 scatterbrains and
    scaredy-cats 98
39 wait on the Lord 101
40 hide and seek 103

41 what's your message? 105
42 The art of "clean-living" 107
43 God the gardener 110
44 juke-box Jesus? 112
45 treasured 114
46 genuine Jesus 116
47 Babel-builders 119
48 reality-check 121
49 superheroes are human 123
50 the Lamb of God 125
    The ABC of becoming a
    Christian 128

the power of prayer

"The prayer of a person living right with God is
something powerful to be reckoned with"
[James 5:16 MSG]

True story believe it or not. One summers day, when I was fourteen, I was
getting all hyped up at an open air service because we were reaching out to
tourists in "sunny Newcastle". But as our Church was setting up the rain
started lashing down. It poured from the heavens like nothing ordinary! There
was thunder and lightening, the full works. It was as if God hadn't spared a
single drop of rain. My smile quickly turned to a frown as people started
making a quick dash for their cars. How could we preach Christ if no-one was
listening?

Our pastor sadly said if the rain didn't stop in a matter of minutes we
would have to pack up and head home. Huddling under an umbrella I prayed
with all my heart "Lord, stop the rain" the split second I said "amen" the rain
stopped. Just like that. Not another drop left heavens storehouse. Breathing
a prayer of thanks I looked up into the sky and saw a break in the clouds
above the promenade. On the horizon of the sea I could see the lightening
and hear the thunder but it kept its distance. *The power of prayer*. Awesome.

This reminds me of a miracle-prayer that Elijah prayed on Mount Carmel with all his might. I'd have a quick flick to 1 Kings 18:16-39 if I were you. Here's the jist of the story. The prophets of Baal had a wee bit of rivalry going with Elijah so they had a prayer shout-out to their gods. But there was no answer, not a peep. Baal must have "bailed" on them! Then it was Elijah's turn to step up to the challenge. He poured lorry-loads of water on the altar until it was soaking and sopping wet. Kind of gives the impression he thinks it's nothing more than a walk in the park, doesn't it?

1 Kings 18:36-37 (NIV) tells the tale, "O Lord, God of Abraham, Isaac and Israel, let it be known today that you are God in Israel and that I am your servant and have done all these things at your command. Answer me, O LORD, answer me, so these people will know that you, O LORD, are God, and that you are turning their hearts back again." You can guess what happened next. God answered, speedily! Fire fell. What is God asking of you? To believe. Nothing more. Nothing less. Pray believing, pray with a purpose. Matthew 21:22, "and all things you ask in prayer, believing, you will receive." Pretty neat verse. Why don't you put it to the test?

THINK UPON THESE THINGS

Prayer: get to the heart of the matter and pray from the heart.

PRAYER

ALMIGHTY GOD I pray that You would teach me to pray - passionately, persistently and powerfully...

_____

_____

_____

God of the impossible

"none of you can get by with blowing your own horn before God.... If you're going to blow a horn, blow a trumpet for God"
(1 Corinthians 1:29, 31 MSG)

Do you ever have days were you feel like you're the biggest nobody that ever walked the earth? Unnoticed. Unloved. Overlooked. Good for nobody and good for nothing. Well here's a God-send with your name on it, *you're spot on*. You are a nobody! Yes, you heard me right. You are a nobody. Thank God! Why? Because **God loves to use nobodies to be a somebody for Him!** It somehow makes sense, doesn't it?

Now before you think to yourself that you aren't worth a single cent, wait until you hear this. You're of unspeakable worth to God. He chose you, "long before he laid down earth's foundations, he had us in mind, had settled on us as the focus of his love" [Ephesians 1:4 MSG]. Never ever dare to think that God writes you off as rubbish. He loves you and that's that, there's no question about it!

Our God is the God of the impossible! He can do the impossible and use us for His glory. Wow. Permanently etch this verse on your brain, "I don't see many of "the brightest and the best" among you... Isn't it obvious that God deliberately chose men and women that the culture overlooks and exploits and abuses, chose these "nobodies" to expose the hollow pretensions of the "somebodies"?" (1 Corinthians 1:26-28 MSG).

Being blunt here, I am a nobody. I could rhyme off a fair few folk who have pretty much written me off as waste, but do you know what? I couldn't care less because they're dead right. I can't make it on my own; that's where God steps in and takes over. There is a long list of losers in the Bible who were in the same muddle as some of us modern-day mess-ups. For a start Jonah ran helter-skelter from God. Thomas doubted beyond belief. Peter was more of a stumbling block than a rock. And to top it all Paul saw himself as being "chief of sinners", bumping off every believer he came across. But none of that seemed to stop them, did it? Actually, I'd go as far as saying that it spurred them on.

That's what I love about my Father-God! He doesn't chose to adopt His children because they can give a three-point sermon, pray for hours on end or be perfect little angels. Do you know how I know this? Because otherwise He would never have chosen me! He chose us because He loves us and **He can use us for His glory.** He can mould us and make us more like Jesus.

PRAYER

Lord, I thank You that You made me a nobody so that I can be a somebody for You and Your glory...

_____

_____

POINT TO PONDER?

Do you ever feel weak-willed or worthless? If you do find your true worth in God. He can work wonders with your weaknesses.

back to basics

"Whatever He tells you, do it"
(John 2:5 MSG)

QUESTION

Is it just me or have we complicated our faith? Am I the only person on the planet who thinks that we've made a mess of it? Do you agree or disagree?

_____

Faith is so simple. So childlike. Some of my earliest memories are of God. Praying on my knees by my bed at night. Chatting to my Child-Minder. Reading His Story-book. Introducing my friends to my Closest Companion. *Never regretting the past, living for that day, never freaking out about the future.* Never trying to storm His Throne-room, leaving it all to Him.

Why have we made something so trouble-free so troublesome? **Why have we made something so clear-cut so complicated?** Why have we made something so straightforward so full of twists and turns? All He asks of us is to trust Him. Plain and simple. No somersaults or cartwheels thrown in, just walking with God. No show, no parade. I wish we would get back to basics. Let's hear what Luke 18:17 [MSG] has to say, "Unless you accept God's kingdom in the simplicity of a child, you'll never get in."

Some days I find myself wishing things were like how they used to be between God and me. I want nothing more than to be able to climb into my Fathers lap and rest a while, not rushing around trying to do one hundred and one chores to satisfy the "god of religious activity and death of true spirituality". I wish I could read His Word out of pure curiosity once again, desperate to find Jesus hidden between the pages, rather than box Him in a Bible study out of little more than a sense of obligation. Think about it, a child throws itself from a height into its parents arms with absolutely no thought. Now that's what I call trust! That's the way it should be with God and me.

QUESTION

How do you and God get on? Has your relationship changed in any way?

_____

_____

Here's another thing. I wish we would just take note of what God's saying and take action. You probably think this is a little "over the top" but it needs to be said. Stop trying to out-do God and *just do what He says*. No pause. No questions. Just do it. I hesitated when God told me to start up a girls Bible study. Snowed under with school work I tried weighing things up, could I take it on? Could I squeeze it in? I analysed, probed and pondered. Not for long though, God jumped in and answered me. Here's what He said, "Connie, just do it." And I did. **Like a child obeys its Father, that's the way faith was designed to be.**

BIBLE BONES

"The Lord protects those of childlike faith" (Psalm 116:6 NLT). Is your faith childlike, or childish? God wants an honest answer.

PRAYER

Father-God I've been so childish wandering from Your way, I want to get back to where I belong. So here I am, sitting at Your feet in Your Throne room... Thanks Papa for Your patience, I'm here to stay...

perfect plan

"I know what I'm doing. I have it all planned out—plans to take care of you, not abandon you, plans to give you the future you hope for"
(Jeremiah 29:11 MSG)

What do you think God's plan for you is? Any idea? Pretty tough question, huh? Do you know what, it doesn't matter what you think His plan for you in the future is. It only matters what His plan for you today is. Makes sense, right?

God taught me a rather tough, but much-needed life-lesson one day. I was

QUESTION

What does God want of you? Where are you right now in your life?

_____

_____

sitting in a daze, like I do, just day-dreaming about all the cool stuff I wanted to do for God in years to come. I had it all mapped out, and boy was it a packed schedule! I even had time-limits set on serving, now that's what I call limiting the Lord! Anyway, here's what God had to say about my scheming, "Connie, did I tell you any of that?" Needless to say my day-dream was cut short, I figured God doesn't care much about what we want to do for Him when we're "all grown up". God wants us to **focus on the present** rather than day dreaming about what may or may not happen in years to come.

Time is precious; don't waste it pondering what you want to do for God someday... What's ahead is safe in God's hands. We should leave it at that. No fussing or fretting. Just relax, God's in charge. Focus on the here and now and God will take care of the rest. He will take care of you, just like He took care of the Prophet Jeremiah. Now Jeremiah definitely didn't have it easy. He was a man with a broken heart, his spirit was crushed by the very people God sent him to witness to. But Jeremiah kept on following God's way anyway. Why? Because he knew that God's ways are better. Far better.

Do you want to know something really exciting? *God has you where He wants you...* how cool is that?! God had placed you according to His perfect plan. You fit into His jigsaw puzzle plan snugly! Yea it may be tough or trying, you may want to dig in your heels, throw a wobbly or even storm out at times but just remember, "God has us where he wants us... All we do is **trust him** enough to **let him do it**" [Ephesians 2:7 MSG]. Focus in on this, it's only ever well with you when you're doing God's will. You may not understand at the time or see Him working it out but just trust Him. After all, He is God, He knows what He's doing.

POINT TO PONDER?

What do you think God's plan for you is, TODAY? What in the world are you waiting for?! Hop to it!

PRAYER

Dear Jesus, show me what You want me to do so that I can't hide from it- set an open door before me...

don't just dream it, do it!

"make the most of every opportunity"
[Colossians 4:5 NLT]

When I was a kid I used to dream big. And I mean big! Now I'm not talking about daydreams; I'm talking giant dreams. I dreamed about serving God in a big way with the little I've got. Now I'm a little older I don't dream anymore. I live it. My worst nightmare would be of me not living out what God has laid on my heart, and not playing my part.

Don't just dream it, do it! With God it can be more than a dream, it can be reality. You don't believe me? Well I have confidence that some dreams are sent from Heaven. Things I dreamt as a child are coming true. I dreamed that God would speak through me, that I

> QUESTION
>
> *Are you playing your part?*
>
> _____
>
> _____

would be a pen in His hand. I never forgot it, holding it in my heart. My dreams lay dormant year after year until not too long ago when I was sitting on the bus God sent me a wee reminder. I was reading a book about a handful of women who took up the challenge to change the world for God, and I thought back to the day where God dropped a dream into my head, and wrote it on my heart.

Now, me being me talk to myself all the time in my head, "I wish I could write a book!" was my heart-cry that day. The Spirit spoke, "well, what's stopping you?" I was gob-smacked. I couldn't even answer Him. I couldn't think of anything that was holding me back. Nothing seemed too big a deal to get in the way of picking up a pen and paper. Yeah, sure I was going to do my A Levels in a couple of months but could I really let my dream pass me by? So I said "yes." Do you know why? Because I'm not only a dreamer, I'm a doer. It wasn't a delusion from the devil but a God-goal that I'm working towards. I hope you take a leaf out of my book and don't just dream it but go for it. **Make the most of every opportunity and the Lord will make the most out of you.**

QUESTION	POINT TO PONDER?
Is your all at His altar? How can we hold back even an ounce of ourselves when God didn't hold back His Son? How can we give our little when God gave His lot?	*Are you a dreamer? Or a DOER? Go on, make the most of what you've got! Never ever let anything stand in your way of serving Jesus.*

are we limiting the Lord?

"You've pushed Me to the limit"
(Jeremiah 6:8 MSG)

Christian bubbles are bad. We can't seem to see past them. No matter what the world throws at us we have something else, something better. It's as if we've taken the wee tune "whatever you can do I can do better" to the extreme. It's a competition that the world hasn't a hope of coming out as top-dog in.

We think that we don't need the world, we can live without them. But you see, they need us, they can't live without us or they will die without Jesus. Scary stuff. That's the last thing we want to see happen. Just think about that for a minute. If they die without Jesus because we are bubbling them out their blood is on our hands. Their loss, our fault. Eek!

Here's another thought; do you know that it is actually possible for us Christians to live outside the Church walls?! Being serious here! That may sound a little silly and a little obvious but it has to be said. God isn't confined to the Church building so why do we confine ourselves? *By curbing ourselves we are caging God.* It's like we have Him imprisoned, He can only go so far and that's the height of it. It's like we've locked Him in a cell and thrown away the key. **Why do we restrict His power over our lives? Why do we limit His love?** Stop pushing God to the limit and just *let Him loose in your life!*

Now we all know that Jesus had a thing or two to say about Church, but let's just home in on what He whispered without words. Jesus definitely wasn't one for cliques. If you wanted to hunt Him down when He walked this earth I doubt you would find Him in the Temple. I think he would be found sitting chilling in the marketplace, out walking the roads, or perhaps soaking up the sun on the seashore. And because God is found just as much, if not more, in the world as in the Church we should remember that our mission field is wherever we walk.

So if you want to escape the Christian bubble follow Jesus' lead, get to it and get out there! Mix and mingle, Christian and non-Christian alike. Meet up for a quick coffee with your friends, or take time out to sit on a park bench and chat to the lonely lady. Jesus kicked back in the boat with His disciples so why don't you have a wee get-together or take a road trip? Think about it, then act on it.

Or, if none of that takes your fancy you could just play it safe. But count this as your one and only warning, **a "safe" lifestyle keeps a lost world lost!** God saved us so that He could save the world. We are meant to be messengers of His Message. **Follow Jesus out of your comfort zone** and carry the Message to the lost.

QUESTION

Who are you going to share the Message with today? Be bold, who will it be?

_____

_____

PRAYER

Jesus, every day all around me people are dying to meet You, but I keep my mouth shut. If I don't act quickly it could be too late for some souls. Make me move, help me to carry this Message to those who don't know You...

BIBLE BONES

"To those who are perishing, we are a dreadful smell of death and doom. But to those who are being saved, we are a life-giving perfume" (2 Corinthians 2:16 NLT). Let God loose in your life, spread a little love, spread a little Life. Turn their darkness into daylight!

stealing centre-stage

"play actors... They get applause, true, but that's all they get"
[Matthew 6:2 MSG]

Let's pretend this life is a little like a stage performance, with a twist. You're living in a land of "make-believe" if you think because it's your life you're the leading-lady or the leading-lad. You don't call the shots, God does. Always has, always will. Never forget that Jesus is the leading man in this stage show; we're just the supporting roles. Unfortunately we're pretty prone to forgetting this fact. Do you know, when we prance and parade about the stage expecting an applause we're not only making fools of ourselves, we're fooling ourselves. Matthew 3:11 [MSG] puts Jesus in His place, centre-stage, He's "the main character in this drama". We're just meant to make God look good-**to God be the glory!**

Here's our downfall in life. We get distracted by the glitz and the glamour all too easily, the sparkles and the sequins take our eyes off our Saviour. We forget Who this Divine drama is all about. Its not about trying to make something of ourselves, its all about shining the spotlight on Jesus. Here's what happens when we forget to do our duty. When Jesus is standing centre-stage we get all starry-eyed and shove Jesus out of the limelight. Don't try and steal Jesus' centre-spot; its not your place. When you realise that God is our everything nothing else matters. Who cares if we don't get the credit?

QUESTION

Are you shining the spotlight on yourself? If the answer is "yes", what are you going to do about it? Here's another thing to think about, in your life who takes the lead?

_____

_____

Here's what Matthew 6:1 (MSG) has to say about us trying to steal the show "It might be good theatre, but the God who made you won't be applauding." And if God doesn't give you a clap and a pat on the back nothing else matters at the end of the day. Now that's a dead cert. This has got to be one of my biggest worries, forgetting my script and harping on about "me me me" rather than Father, Son and Spirit. Being seen as being a light in the darkness can have its drawbacks you know. The focus can so easily shift from the Saviour to the servant. Bad move. I always have to ask myself when people look at me- is all they see me or can they see the God-glow inside of me?

Pray that you wouldn't get star-struck with yourself, but that Jesus would be the Star that guides you home. Pray that you would fix your focus on Him. And while you're at it, give a special prayer shout-out for your spiritual fathers and mothers in the faith, that they wouldn't flick the switch so the spotlight is shining on themselves instead of on Jesus. Sure, He's the Light of the world so He deserves all the limelight He can get, right?

PRAYER

Father I'm so sorry for being self-centred. From now on in may my life revolve around You! I'm stepping off to the sidelines, take centre-stage...

THINK UPON THESE THINGS

This life, it's not about me, it's all about You, Jesus. Give God His rightful role, don't keep Him behind the scenes.

for the glory of God

"Good work! You did your job well. From now
on be my partner"
[Matthew 25:23 MSG]

QUESTION

*What did you want to do when you were young? Be a teacher?
Learn to play guitar? Travel the world? Or be a "stay at home"
mum? Write down your thoughts.*

_____

_____

Serving the Saviour doesn't have to lead you on a mission in a far off country.
It can start on your street. Only God knows where it could lead you! You could
teach those around you about Jesus through your word and your walk, soul-
sing as you play your part in Sunday morning worship, travel with Him on your
journey through life and *live your love* for God out at home bringing your kids
to Christ. God gave you aspirations for one soul reason. So that you would
chase them. **Don't let your dreams slip out of sight**, run after them for dear

life! Never ever ever forget this, "God makes their dreams come true" (Psalm 14:5 MSG) He can do the same for you!

When I get Home I want to hear my Father say "Well done, my good and faithful servant. You have been faithful in handling this small amount, so now I will give you many more responsibilities. Let's celebrate together!" (Matthew 25:23 NLT). I don't have to do anything out of the ordinary to *make God smile.* Just follow through with what I was born to do.

To prove my point let's take a look at some of the "heroes of faith".

You would expect God to have placed them in some pretty important places, right?

Now that's where you're wrong.

Let's start with Daniel; God led him to a lions' lair.

And what about Joseph, and Paul; come to think of it, they served their time in a cell.

And John the Baptist, he spent his time wandering around the wilderness.

Point proven.

If God's purpose for you is to serve in the back end of nowhere in a bog standard job, do everything **for the glory of God** and you will be surprised what He can do! **He can turn your little into a lot!**

QUESTION

Can you think of any other "heroes" or "heroines"? Try and think outside the box.

_____

_____

QUESTION

Where are you in your walk with God? What could He be calling you to do?

_____

_____

_____

BIBLE BONES

"If anyone speaks, he should do it as one speaking the very words of God. If anyone serves, he should do it with the strength God provides, so that in all things God may be praised through Jesus Christ. To him be the glory and the power for ever and ever. Amen" [1 Peter 4:11 NIV]. To God be the glory! We should be God-honouring in all that we do, what will you do for Him today?

PRAYER

Father God may everything that I do be for Your glory. When I stand before You on Judgement day I want to see You smile...

the Light of Life

"You're here to be light, bringing out the God-colours in the world. **God is not a secret to be kept.** We're going public with this, as public as a city on a hill. If I make you light-bearers, you don't think I'm going to hide you under a bucket, do you?"
[Matthew 5:14-15 MSG]

We're born to be the light of the world, not the light within our Christian-clique. The last thing that God wants is for us to just shine the light for ourselves and turn a blind eye to those who can't see in the dark. We're called to carry the Torch wherever we go, so that the lost can follow the Light. *How else are they meant to find their Saviour in the shadows unless someone shows them the way?*

If you think about it the phrase "under a bucket" could be interpreted as being the Christian bubble. The Light of Life will die if we smother its flame, which we tend to do these days. Do exactly what Matthew 5:16 [MSG] says, "Now that I've put you there on a hilltop, on a light stand—shine!" **Shine like the Son!**

You want to know how to put this into practice? Well, here's a challenge for you. Do a random act of kindness today. You can do anything you want. Invite the kid who is bubbled out of the lunch bunch to sit with you and share a sandwich. Take your

neighbours dog for a dander when they are bed bound. Help your dad sweep the street or let your mum put her feet up for an hour or two as you do the spring-cleaning. Go on, I dare you! When you go the extra mile the Light of Life shines ever-bright in their eyes! Just think about it.

You could take it from a different angle, and compare the bucket that we hide our light under to the Church building. It's only by "By opening up to others, you'll prompt people to open up with God" [Matthew 5:16 MSG]. We have to bring the Light outside of the Church so everyone can see that "I am the light of the world. Whoever follows me will never walk in darkness, but will have the light of life" [John 8:12 NIV]. When we don't shine like the Son it's as if we have Him boxed, labelled and bubbled. **He can only do so much. He can only light as many lives as we let Him.**

BIBLE BONES

"I am sending you to them to open their eyes so that they may turn away from darkness to the light"
[Acts 26:17-18 NCV].

heavy heart

"Open up before God, keep nothing back"
(Psalm 37:5 MSG)

There are countless days in my calendar where I feel like I am being teased by troubles and crushed by concerns. I'm a born worrier. I worry about anything and everything, half of which isn't even any of my business to be worrying about!

What I have to remind myself again and again is that God is only a prayer away, I can go to my Heavenly Father whenever I have fragile feelings or a hurt heart. 1 John 3:20 (MSG) gets right to the heart of the matter, "God is greater than our worried hearts". He is bigger-than. He is a Heart-Healer. The words unfixable and impossible aren't found in His dictionary.

QUESTION

Are you a prayer worrier or a prayer warrior? Take some time on this one. Be honest and open up...

I'm ashamed to say that I go through trust-battles with God all the time. When I should really let God fight for me I am out there on my own swinging my sword and getting nowhere. Philippians 4:6-7 (MSG) has some rather helpful advice, "Don't fret or worry. Instead of worrying, pray. Let petitions and praises shape your worries into prayers, letting God know your concerns. Before you know it, a sense of God's wholeness, everything coming together for good, will come and settle you down. It's wonderful what happens when Christ displaces worry at the centre of your life." When faced with problems pray away!

When I am disheartened God reminds me that He wants my all, worries are part of the parcel! Our motto should be to "Live carefree before God; He is most careful with you" (1 Peter 5:7 MSG). Hand over your heart and He will hand over His happiness.

THINK UPON THESE THINGS

Quick, grab a pen and paper and scribble down all your fears and phobias. Write down absolutely everything that's bugging your brain, no matter how small it may seem. Done it? Now, bring them before God's Throne and leave your luggage there! Rip up your worries and throw them in the bin, because at the end of the day your worries are just a waste of time! Live life light, lay down your load at the foot of the cross.

PRAYER

Heavenly Father help me to hold nothing back from You as I come before the Throne of Grace...

a God-hug

""The minute I said, "I'm slipping, I'm falling," your love, God, took hold and held me fast. When I was upset and beside myself, you calmed me down and cheered me up"
(Psalm 94:16 MSG)

God knows you inside out. He knows when you're having a bad day and need cheering up. One day I was having a lousy day, things just weren't going my way. I was feeling like a river run dry. I knew exactly were David was coming from when he said "my soul longs for You, as a parched land" (Psalm 143:6 NASB). So God decided to do something about it and send a little aid. I was doing my devotions and suddenly God popped a tune in my head to take my mind off everything-that-had-gone-wrong and focus on everything-that-He-had-done-right.

QUESTION

Are you thirsty for more? Have a read at Psalm 63...

It goes like this, "Saviour of my soul, Jesus you make me whole. Fountain in a thirsty land, all goodness flows from Your hand. Your loving-kindness is better than life, and in the presence of Your wings I will rejoice, I will rejoice." It simply sums up who God is, doesn't it? **Thank God** that He is our Fountain whenever we run dry and need revived, "My soul thirsts for You; my flesh longs for You in a dry and thirsty land where there is no water" [Psalm 63:1 NKJV].

Thank God that He quenches our thirst, He satisfies our souls. **Thank God** He knows just what we need and when we need it. Thank God that His "lovingkindness is better than life" [Psalm 63:3 NKJV]. *Thank God* that He upholds you when you feel that you're about to buckle under the pressure. Thank Him for "God-aid" that He sends by prayer-mail (air-mail). Sing it out, "in the shadow of Your wing I will rejoice" [Psalm 63:7 NKJV]. **Thank God** we've got something to shout about!

QUESTION
What are you thankful for? Make a long list...
_____
_____
_____
_____
_____

THINK UPON THESE THINGS

When you're feeling as dry as a dessert Jesus can saturate your soul with His goodness. Soak it in and sponge it up!

PRAYER
Father when I feel like everything is falling apart may I cling on to You...
_____
_____
_____

"the hall of nobodies"

"Quick, God, I need your helping hand!"
(Psalm 12:1 MSG)

Something struck me when I was reading Hebrews 11 a wee while ago, a pretty awesome chapter if you ask me. Did you know that "the hall of fame" is actually just a bunch of nobodies? They weren't anything special. Being serious now. They weren't "high and mighty". Before you go any further read the chapter from start to finish, see if you can spot any "nobodies"?

"The hall of nobodies" is crammed full of men and women who twigged on to something special, they knew it was impossible to get through life on their own. They knew they needed a helping hand so they gave themselves up to God. If you do your best God is sure to do the rest! This bunch of misfits came to realise that **with God on their side nothing was impossible**. They simply trusted that if God could do all things He could use them.

I know for sure that if God put me in charge of picking His army I would have steered well clear of the "heroes" and "heroines" of faith that He handpicked. After all, Peter was a fisherman. David was a shepherd boy. Mary was a teenage mother. And Rahab was a prostitute, no way near worthy of a place in God's palace by our standards. You may be a school kid or student, but **what does that have to do with it?** Don't let it stop you. God isn't an ageist so why should you be? God makes it crystal clear, *"don't let anyone put you down because you're young."* (1 Timothy 4:12 MSG). Including yourself! God has big plans for you, He handpicked you with a purpose. Don't let anything get in the way of you serving God.

People used to look down their noses at me because they thought I couldn't possibly know a thing about this God-life, because after all I was only a kid wasn't I? Wrong! That's a lie straight from the devil's lips, don't believe it for a single second. God can use any one, from the oldest to the very youngest, if only they wake up and realise it. Go on give it a shot, join the God-squad! One day you may have your picture in the "hall of nobodies" in Heaven, you never know!

BIBLE BONES

"Let no one despise your youth, but be an example to the believers in word, in conduct, in love, in spirit, in faith, in purity" (1 Timothy 4:12 NKJV).

PRAYER

Father, I'm Yours. Have Your way in me! I give You my all, it may not be much but it's all I have to offer. Use me for Your glory...

the counterfeit christ uncovered

"He said to them, But who do you [yourselves] say that I am?"
(Matthew 16:15 Amplified)

There's a manmade myth that has somehow snuck its way into Sunday school. When I was a kid I always imagined Jesus with beautiful blue eyes, spotless skin and not a hair out of place. When I coloured in my cartoon-Christ I always dressed Jesus in a blue beauty pageant sash and a flowing white gown. How wrong could I have been. *That's not my Jesus.* That's the complete opposite of who Jesus is and what He stands for.

From the pasty portraits in my picture books I got the notion that Jesus was a bit of a mama's boy, a big softy who wouldn't say anything too snappy or sharp in case He offended us in any way. Not so, that's most definately not my Jesus! Yes, my Jesus can be soft-spoken and gentle at times but He can be fiery and fierce when He wants to.

Before He opened my eyes to who He really was I always thought that Jesus was a happy-go-lucky sort of guy, with His head high in the sky. There's a major problem with picturing Jesus as a bit of a hippie, skipping merrily through a meadow singing sweet songs to sheep and making daisy chains.

He only lives in our imagination. Now I'm not saying that Jesus never existed, He's real alright! I'm just saying that *we've created a counterfeit christ*. My Jesus is not a jester or a joker.

If Jesus walked the earth today I think He would be least likely found floating about with His head in the clouds. I think He would be out and about saving and satisfying souls! He would be casting out demons, raising the dead, preaching to the poor and standing up to the school bullies. That's my Jesus!

This is what it all comes down to, in Matthew 16 Jesus was walking and talking with His disciples and He threw a question out there, "who do people say the Son of Man is?" (Matthew 16:13 Amplified). John the Baptist, Elijah, Jeremiah or one of the prophets were what the people believed Him to be. Then it got interesting, Jesus turned to Simon Peter and threw this one in his face, "who do you say that I am? "Matthew 16:15 NIV). **Forget what everyone else thinks of Him, what about you?** Peter confessed Christ, here's what he proclaimed, "You are the Christ, the Son of the living God" (Matthew 16:16 NIV). Can you say the same?

POINT TO PONDER?

What about you? Who do you say Jesus is? This has got to be the most important answer you'll ever give. Take the time to reflect on Matthew 16:13-20 before you make up your mind.

God's plan prevails

"Don't look for shortcuts to God... The way to life- to
God!- is vigorous and requires total attention"
[Matthew 7:13-14 MSG]

There's no point putting up a fight. God always wins. Always. If you kick up a
fuss and "do a Jonah" you had better make an about turn... and pronto! God
is on your tail! There is no running from what God has in store for you. Check
out the book of Jonah. Before you read another word open your Bible to
Jonah 1 and read the chapter from start to finish, study it in-depth.

Once you've read it you'll realise that it talks about Jonah dashing off in
the opposite direction from God, trying his hardest to run "as far from God as
he could get" [Jonah 1:2 MSG]. Here's what happened, God told Jonah to get
up and go, to lead the city of Ninevah to repentance, but Jonah dug in his
heels in protest. Sounds unbelievable but here's what happened next, "Jonah
rose up to flee... from the presence of the Lord" [Jonah 1:3 NASB]. Now we
both know that that's quite the impossibility. You can never, no never, take
flight from the Father.

Needless to say God had a trick up His sleeve. "God sent a huge storm"
[Jonah 1:4 MSG] to bring Jonah back to where he belonged. God will grab
your attention, you will be sitting up and paying attention in no time! There's
only one thing for it, only one way to get yourself out of this pickle... **total
surrender**. I can't emphasise this enough, this is the turning point!

The moment you surrender the storm in your soul stops "He stilled the storm to a whisper; the waves of the sea were hushed" (Psalm 107:29 NIV). As soon as Jonah sacrificed his self-seeking soul the wild and rowdy sea stilled. You may be thinking that surrender is about giving up and giving in, but it isn't. It's about giving yourself over to God.

Never forget that "a man's heart plans his way, but the Lord directs his steps." (Proverbs 16:9 NKJV). As soon as you're off the road He has laid before you He sets off after you because He knows the best route Home, you haven't found a short-cut. You can't out-smart God, it's just another detour. "I will guide you along the best pathway for your life" (Psalm 32:8 NLT), God knows what He's doing, trust Him. Let God bring His plan to pass. Don't pass on His plan.

BIBLE BONES

"Whether you turn to the right or to the left, your ears will hear a voice behind you, saying, "This is the way; walk in it" " (Isaiah 30:21 NIV). Prick up your ears and listen out for the Lord; He won't leave you stranded.

PRAYER

Father I want Your will, I really do- help me to trust Your judgements...

_____

_____

_____

seek out to serve

"I do not ask You to take them out of the world,
but to keep them from the evil one. They are not
of the world, even as I am not of the world"
[John 17:15-16 NASB]

QUESTION

*You would think that with God on our side there is nothing stopping
us from taking over the world for Jesus, or is there?*
Carefully consider this question.

Here's my slant on it, if you're having a down-day there are the easiest things to put you back on track. Think of Christian music. It makes you feel all warm and fuzzy inside, driving away the blues. Nothing beats a sing-song eh? Hang on a tick, it's as if we don't have to listen to what the world listens to anymore, because its tunes are tasteless and tacky, right? We can just drown out the drone. It doesn't just stop at music. You don't have to go too far to find Christian key rings, DVDs, fridge magnets, place mats and even socks! It's as if we have created a self-sufficient world. Yikes.

The sad thing is **the world can't compete with the Christian culture we have created.** We don't even need to rub shoulders with the world anymore, you can hide out in a Christian corner all day. There's Christian schools, bookstores, cafes, and youth groups. We're cornering ourselves off.

Turn with me to Luke 19, it tells a tale of Zaccheus, a midget of a man, who God-fearing folks steered well clear off because he was a greedy-guts and a money-grabbing tax-collector. The story goes like so, Jesus was passing through the city of Jericho when masses flooded and flocked to see Him. Seeing that Zaccheus was lacking in height, to say the least, he ran on ahead of the crowd and scrambled up a sycamore tree. Now here's where the pious people were shaken to their senses, Jesus made time for the man they shunned and scorned.

Luke 19:5 (NKJV) puts it this way. When Jesus was walking by He looked up and saw Zacchaeus sitting in the treetops and said to him, "Zacchaeus, make haste and come down, for today I must stay at your house." I'm sure they didn't see that one coming. With that they grumbled "He has gone to be a guest with a man who is a sinner" " (Luke 19:7 NKJV). We've all been there and done that. Admit it. We've been slagging when we've absolutely no right to. There's only one person on this planet who has a right to judge, and that's Jesus. And guess what, He doesn't frown down upon them. He looks them straight in the eye and whispers those three little words. I hope He's taught you a lesson today.

Recently I've woken up and realised that Jesus had a pretty good point when He said "the Son of Man has come to seek and to save that which was lost" (Luke 19:10 NKJV). **Seek out to serve, that's what we're called to do.** Seek and serve. If you missed that one here it is again in the book of Mark, "those who are well have no need of a physician, but those who are sick. I did not come to call the righteous, but sinners to repentance" (Mark 2:17 NKJV). Let's face it, they need us, because they need Jesus.

So here's what we've learned today. We're so equipped to go and conquer the world for Jesus, but there's one thing stopping us. We're trapped in a bubble. We can't get out, and the world can't get in. Luke 9:3 (MSG) sums it up in a nutshell, "Don't load yourselves up with equipment. Keep it simple; **you are the equipment**."

POINT TO PONDER?

Are you seeking out ways in which to serve? Stop serving yourself, get out there- GO! Remember the Great Commission, turn to it - Matthew 28:19-20.

PRAYER

Burst this bubble! Jesus I want to be free to follow You into my mission field...

fake Pharisees

"You're like manicured grave plots,
grass clipped and the flowers bright, but
six feet down it's all rotting bones and worm-
eaten flesh. People look at you
and think you're saints, but beneath
the skin you're total frauds"
(Matthew 23:27-28 MSG)

Beware! There are modern-day hypocrites living amongst us. Chances are you have met one or two in your time. They build their own platforms and blow their own trumpets. They are godless rather than godly. If anyone doesn't quite make their mark they are tossed aside and trampled underfoot. If you ever meet one I suggest you make an about-turn and scarper.

But why is it that they are so hard to spot? Why is it that they are so hard to figure out? They have a few tricks up their sleeves for sure, they disguise their blemishes by sticking on fake smiles and speaking sweet words. When your back is turned they will spill your secrets like a sewer. These phoneys paraded around, teaching whatever takes their fancy and looking down their noses at anyone and everyone who isn't as blue-blooded as they are. They make it out that they're in a purity-pageant but they are really in a criminal-carnival.

Having said all that, I feel a sense of conviction. Maybe, just maybe, I need to hear this message more than anyone else? I can be horribly hypocritical at times, it's as if I've disowned the Way and trekked along my own track. I would go as far as saying that Jesus would be down-right ashamed of me and my actions. Something God has brought to my attention in recent days is that if I'm ashamed of the Gospel I'm a shame to the Gospel. Pretty hard-hitting eh?

So if I hang my head and can't even look someone in the eye and tell them I love Jesus, I'm a phoney and a fake. I can go for days on end without even so much as speaking His name, let alone bringing Him into the conversation. I really truly mean it when I say I'm madly and deeply in love with Jesus, so why can't I share Him from sunrise to sunset with anyone and everyone who crosses my path? I just don't make much sense at times.

Wrapping it up, there's only one way to figure out a counterfeit Christian, watch their every move. Their walk fouls their faith. They talk the talk but stagger and stumble rather than walking the walk, "They talk a good line, but they don't live it. They don't take it into their hearts and live it out in their behaviour. It's all spit-and-polish veneer." [Matthew 23:3 MSG]. I'm serious when I say this, **there's a world of difference between being religious and being righteous.** Which one are you?

QUESTION

Are you religious? Or righteous?

_____

_____

_____

Watch out, fake Pharisees are never too far away. These sinister saints can drag you down and pollute your faith if you aren't too careful. I would take a good long look in the Mirror though, and see if a fake Pharisee is staring back at you. You never know; they could be closer than you think.

BIBLE BONES

"Woe to you, scribes and Pharisees, pretenders (hypocrites)! For you clean the outside of the cup and of the plate, but within they are full of extortion (prey, spoil, plunder) and grasping self-indulgence. You blind Pharisee! First clean the inside of the cup and of the plate, so that the outside may be clean also" (Matthew 23:25-26 Amplified). Say sorry for your sins, and be specific!

Read through Matthew 23:1-39 and reflect. How do you see yourself? Open your eyes!

ask in accordance

"when you assume the posture of prayer,
remember that it's not all asking"
[Mark 11:22 MSG]

Prayer has got to be one of the greatest gifts God has ever given us. We can have a God-chat about absolutely anything, anytime, anywhere. Yet we abuse this gift. We treat it like nothing more than a wish-list and expect delivery the very day we send our requests to Heaven. "God gimme this" and "God gimme that" is all we ever think about.

Well you've got something coming, here's the latest newscast- God is not a genie. Get it out of your head. And here's another thing. Don't you dare boss God about. We take orders from Him, not the other way around. Stating the obvious here. God isn't a mystic-magician either. He doesn't wave a magic wand and make all your wishes come true, even if you do say the magic word it won't make much difference. That's not what prayer is about. It isn't about God sending you Mr or Mrs Right, the pretty pony you have always wanted or letting you be the leading role in the school play.

One day when one of my best friends, Laura Gordon, was a kid she hadn't quite got her head around what was the point of prayer. She didn't ask God to feed the starving kids in Africa, or bring world peace, or even that He would help her with her sums or be with granny when she was in hospital. She dared to ask God for a mermaid costume. Yep, you heard me right, a fish-frock. She even had the cheek to tell Him where to leave it. No brownie points for guessing what happened. Nothing. God didn't grant her wish. I hate to nitpick on Gordo though, I have to say she's come on a long way since then, she doesn't pray for frivolous things anymore.

Keep this in mind, *"God will hear our prayers when we ask for what pleases Him"* (1 John 5:14 CEV); we have to ask in accordance with His will. There's no point praying with the purpose to please yourself. You're wasting your time, let alone God's time listening to you chatter on about a load of codswallop. God doesn't deliver prezzies; He packs and parcels promises. That's more than enough to get us by. **Don't confuse Santa Claus with your Saviour.** Big mistake. God doesn't wear a big red suit, but He does wear a smile when you ask for what pleases Him. Never forget it.

BIBLE BONES

"We're able to stretch our hands out and receive what we asked for because we're doing what He said, doing what pleases Him" (1 John 3:21 MSG). Pray with the purpose of pleasing your Heavenly Father. Say sorry for using and abusing the gift of prayer...

the Father's love

"it's time you appreciated God's deep love"
(Psalm 107:43 MSG)

The Father's love. Pretty breathtaking, huh? Let's take a tour of the Bible, the greatest love letter that was ever written, and pinpoint moments in time where God has whispered those three little words over and over again. Let them find a home in your heart. By the end of it your head will be spinning just thinking about His limitless love!

Before you read my ramblings try and describe the Father's Love. If I was you I'd turn to the Gospels to start off with...

To begin with God's love is life-long. "his love lasts" (Psalm 106:1 MSG) and "his love never runs out" (Psalm 107:1 MSG). You can never ever reach the bottom of God's barrelful of blessings, never! He keeps on pouring out His love day in and day out. You are probably thinking His love is bound to dry up sooner or later, think again. His love is unfailing, unshakeable, never-ending. Not only that, His love is lush. God speaks words of love through Hosea 14:4 (MSG) - "I will love them lavishly". You are dearly beloved. **Isn't it a comforting thought that God not only holds you in His hands but in His heart?** Try and get your head around that one!

The Father's love is not only marvellous, it's miraculous. When you think God couldn't possibly top that, take a look at this- the greatest love story of them all. "For God so greatly loved and dearly prized the world that He [even] gave up His only begotten (unique) Son, so that whoever believes in (trusts in, clings to, relies on) Him shall not perish (come to destruction, be lost) but have eternal (everlasting) life" (John 3:16 Amplified).

Just you sit back and soak it in. He's the deliverer of darkness and the destroyer of death. He went to hell and back for you... for you! Just look at it, "Some of you were locked in a dark cell, cruelly confined behind bars... A hard sentence, and your hearts so heavy, and not a soul in sight to help. Then you called out to God in your desperate condition; he got you out in the nick of time. He led you out of your dark, dark cell, broke open the jail and led you out. So thank God for his marvelous love, for his miracle mercy to the children **he loves**" (Psalm 107:10, 12-15 MSG). Don't you forget it; the greatest love story that was ever written was written in the blood of Christ on Calvary. He shed His blood to save your soul. The greatest gift of love that God has ever given us was wrapped in a manger, and nailed to a tree. Now that's Love!

Thank Him for it...

THINK UPON THESE THINGS

The greatest gift of love wasn't found in a stocking, but in a stable. Jesus was a God-send sent to save us from our sins! Praise God!

garbage gift-wrapped

"You're blessed when you feel you've lost what
is most dear to you. Only then can you be
embraced by the One most dear to you"
[Matthew 5:4 MSG]

It looks like there's only one thing for it, doesn't it? You've got to lay down
everything that's dear to you before His throne. Let go of what you're
clutching onto like your life depends on it. Let's face it, it doesn't amount to
much anyway. Sounds obvious but I'm going to go ahead and say it anyway;
our lives depend on God, not garbage. That's the height of all insults, hanging
onto stuff instead of holding onto our Saviour. Here's what you've got to go
and do; empty yourself of earth's rubbish, because that's all it is, the spoil you
thought it was, spoils your life. The moment you lay it down something
amazing happens right before your eyes. You see it for what it really is.
Everything you thought was of worth turns to waste; it withers away there
and then. It was never glam; it was *garbage gift-wrapped*.

I can't say I've mastered this one myself. I've a tendency to try and fill my life with whatever "jewels" and "gems" I can get my hands on. I'm a bit of a magpie so if I see something I want it's as good as mine because I'm out to own it! It could be a relationship, a role, or absolutely anything that makes me let go of God and grab it. Thankfully things were about to take a u-turn as God knew something pretty drastic had to happen.

> **QUESTION**
>
> *What are your prized possessions? Are they of real worth?*
>
> _____
>
> _____
>
> _____

One day He opened my eyes and showed me that it was just junk. It was just second-hand scrap compared to what Jesus had in store for me. Same goes for you!

We've got to get it into our heads that we can't replace Jesus with junk. On one hand we've got a priceless treasure and on the other we've got worthless waste. There's absolutely no comparison in this "competition". We spend all our strength trying to squeeze stuff into a God-shaped hole in our hearts when the solution to this snag is that God fits squarely.

> **QUESTION**
>
> *Is there anything in your life that's competing with Christ?*
>
> _____
>
> _____

You have to be empty for Jesus to fill you. I have to be honest; it's far easier said than done. You have to let go of the hoards of treasure you're building up for yourself here on earth so that *Jesus can fill you to overflowing.* You see, Jesus can't pour riches into hands already full. He can't fill your life until you're clinging onto nothing but Him. God challenged me on this one years ago. He asked me to lay everything before Him and leave it. And I did, because I realised that I had to open up my hands so that God could open up my heart. There was no point holding something back because God couldn't have stepped in and stripped all the second-hand scrap from my life if I put up a fight. Don't let your garbage get in the way of your God. **Open up your hands and open up your heart.** Here's the thing, *everything that you're holding onto is holding you back.*

POINT TO PONDER?

What are you hanging onto like your life depends on it? Will you not give it up? Give it up to God and He will hand over His hoards of happiness.

crimes against Christ

"People conceived and brought into life by
God don't make a practice of sin"
[1 John 3:9 MSG]

QUESTION

*Hate to grill you this early on but I'm going to go ahead
and ask it anyway. Would you die for Jesus?*

_____

_____

Goodness gracious me, that's a great big question! Now before you go and
jump to conclusions I'm not talking about giving up the ghost, I'm talking
about *dying to sin*. Here's the thing, **if you want to be alive to God you've got
to be dead to the world**.

You still think you can have the best of both worlds? Well here's a news
flash for you; you can't dabble in sin and serve God at the same time; you're
just kidding yourself. It's quite the impossibility. 1 John 1:6 [NLT] echoes this,
"we are lying if we say we have fellowship with God but go on living in spiritual

darkness". If you keep on walking in your own way you haven't crucified the flesh, actually you're kind of resurrecting it, bringing it back to life every time you choose to sin instead of serve; yikes, now there's a scary thought. Every time we give in to sin we're raising "the old man" from the dead, and he's killing "the new man". Know what I mean?

1 Peter 2:24 (ESV) turns our attention to Jesus, "He himself bore our sins in his body on the tree, that we might die to sin and live to righteousness." Do you really think that Jesus hasn't a bit of a bother about us raising our "old man" from the dead? Our old life should stay six feet under. Anyway, whatever the devil is throwing in your face to lure you away from your Love is just a passing pleasure at the end of the day. The one thing that will survive with us beyond the grave is our sacrificial service. Only what's done for Jesus will last longer than this life. I don't think I could face Jesus on Judgement Day if I knew I wasn't giving this life a serious shot. How about you?

Let's wrap this up with Galatians 5:24 (NIV), "Those who belong to Christ Jesus have crucified the sinful nature with its passions and desires." We all know that the sinful nature craves what is contrary to the Spirit, Jesus never said this God-life would be easy-going. There's going to be a fierce fight between the flesh and faith. Just remember, **if you are a child of God you can't go on committing crimes against Christ.**

THINK UPON THESE THINGS

If you aren't prepared to die to sin, you will never truly live for Him. It's hard to hear but oh-so true!

free as free can be

"Because of the sacrifice of the Messiah, his blood poured out on the altar of the Cross, **we're a free people**—free of penalties and punishments chalked up by all our misdeeds. And not just barely free, either. Abundantly free!"
(Ephesians 1:7-8 MSG)

Some of you may be thinking that you've strayed so far from God that you can't come back. The devil loves to lie, and that's a biggie. *You are never out of God's reach.* God gives you chance after chance. He doesn't keep a record of how many times He has to bring you back. You can have a clean slate. A fresh start. What's in the past is history. There's freedom in the future. Now here's what I want you to do- just you sit back and soak in these verses, let them still your restless soul...

Psalm 103:12 (NIV) lays bare the heart of God, Forgiveness is His name, **"as far as the east is from the west, so far has he removed our transgressions from us."** As far as Heaven is from Hell, so far as He removed our transgressions from us. He has buried your sins down in the deep, don't dig them up.

"Though your sins are like scarlet, I will make them as white as snow. Though they are red like crimson, I will make them as white as wool" (Isaiah 1:18 NLT). If that hasn't sunk in I'll echo it, your sin-sick soul when washed in the precious blood of the Lamb will be made snowy white!

See, there's no need to worry. God has it covered, with the blood of Christ, **"This is my blood of the covenant, which is poured out for many for the forgiveness of sins."** [Matthew 26:28 NIV]. This is "the full extent of his love" [John 13:1 NIV], the cross of Calvary. Take time out to thank God for Jesus!

"If the Son makes you free, you shall be free indeed" [John 8:36 NKJV]. Jesus bought your freedom with His blood, you aren't a slave to your sin any longer! When the Son makes you free you are free as free can be!

There's no need for you to be guilt-ridden, **"Gone your guilt, your sins wiped out"** [Isaiah 6:6 MSG]. You know God could have wiped us out if He really wanted to, but He didn't. Instead He sent His Son, Jesus, which means "God saves"- **"because he will save his people from their sins"** [Matthew 1:22 MSG].

Thank God that He is **"lavish with forgiveness"** [Isaiah 55:7 MSG]. Praise God He **"rescued us from dead-end alleys and dark dungeons"** [Colossians 1:13 MSG]. There wasn't a tower too tall, a river too wide or a valley too low to keep Him apart from us. He is our Rescuer.

Now, there's no excuse for sinning against God Almighty, but even if the only words of confession are **"God, give mercy. Forgive me, a sinner"** [Luke 18:13 MSG], then it is enough to cover a life-time of sins, if you act on it that is! Take God up on His offer and let Him wash you as white as snow.

THINK UPON THESE THINGS

Don't bring the past into the present, God says forget it, it's history!

miracle-worker

"Ask in prayer, believe that you have
received it, and it will be yours"
(Mark 11:24 NIV)

QUESTION

Do you believe that God has the healing touch today?
It's quite a controversial question, isn't it? What's your
mind on the matter?

_____

_____

When I was fifteen I have to confess I was basically nothing more than a
worn-out workaholic. I slaved away at school, and I didn't give myself any slack
when I got home. I went straight to my studies, burying my head in a book for
hours on end. Unlucky for me I contracted the dreaded mumps, and because
I was dead beat things got pretty complicated. My brother and sister found
the whole situation rather hilarious, nicknaming me "fat face", when in fact it

was far from a joke. (I'm going to name and shame them- Sam and Abi!) Getting back on track, it got to the stage where it had messed up my hearing, and infected a couple of my internal organs. I then contracted post-viral fatigue and was bed bound for several weeks. Not nice.

At times I couldn't even turn the pages of my Bible because I didn't have the strength. It was only when *I felt completely helpless that I finally realised that my help was found in God.* I am not proud of it but here's the naked truth. God had to literally floor me to grab my attention and force me to get my priorities right. God first.

That having been said, somehow, one day I managed to drag myself out of bed and make it to Whitewell Tabernacle. Tears filled my eyes as I didn't even have the energy to sing to my Jesus. After the service I was brought to be prayed for by a couple of the pastors. What happened next will stay with me forever and a day. A simple prayer was said. A prayer of faith. "Believing-prayer will heal you, and Jesus will put you on your feet." (James 5:14-15 MSG) Not a shock that I walked out of Whitewell as right as rain? Luke 1:36 (MSG) gets straight to the point, **"Nothing, you see, is impossible with God."** Let Mark 9:24 (MSG) be your answer, "I believe. Help me with my doubts!"

The Miracle-Worker is just as powerful and present today as He was when He walked on this earth. Take the miracle-story from Luke 8 for example. A women who had been afflicted with hemorrhages for twelve

QUESTION

Why don't you scribble down some miracle-prayers from the Bible? Think upon these things...

_____

_____

years had the guts to go up to Jesus and act out her faith by touching His cloak. It isn't surprising that she was instantly healed. Here's what Jesus had to say to her, "Daughter, you took a risk trusting me, and now you're healed and whole. Live well, live blessed!" (Luke 8:48 MSG). He remains the same; yesterday, today, and forever. He was and is and will always be the God of miracles! Praise God He can work wonders! Always remember to lean on God. He is your *unfailing strength*. Nothing can substitute God Almighty.

THINK UPON THESE THINGS

Do you have faith that prayer works? Put it to the test and God will do the rest!

singled out for something special

"Instead of trusting in our own strength or wits to get out of it, we were forced to trust God *totally*"
[Isaiah 12:1 MSG]

We've got this strange notion stuck in our heads that God just uses the cool kids and all those who don't seem to fit in God shoves off to the side. I honestly don't think that this could be further from the truth!

God doesn't care about superficial skin-deep stuff, those popular kids who make everyone else green with envy God has a much harder time trying to put them to good use. And here's why, they have made a major slip-up along the way and instead of relying on Jesus they have confidence in their own "strength". Wait until you hear this, "Those who fear God get God's attention; they can depend on his strength" [Psalm 147:7 MSG]. *When you lean on the Lord His eyes are on you!*

Take the story of David and Goliath for instance, sit down and study 1 Samuel 17. We all know that things got a little out of hand, it looked like there was going to be a spot of bother. The Israelites were quaking in their boots, but David on the other hand had obviously had his cup of courage that morning because he was raring to go! He had God grinning from ear to ear when he preached this speech, "You come to me with sword, spear, and javelin, but I come to you in the name of the Lord of Heaven's Armies—the God of the armies of Israel... Today the Lord will conquer you" [1 Samuel 17:45-46 NLT]. David had it spot on, He is our strength. *It's those who rely wholly on God who get singled out for something special.*

QUESTION

Have you had your cup of courage today?! Drink deep from the Word of God, go on...

Just incase you don't believe me I'm going to say it again. God doesn't give "a hoot" about whether or not you are talented. I don't have a musical bone in my body, I can't sing or act to save my life, I'm not on a sports team and I'm not a high-flyer in exams but God manages to use me, not in spite of it, but because of it. And the same goes for you, God can use you too! You see, God has an easier time employing people who aren't that big or brainy because they don't make a show of themselves, they **big-up God instead**. Shout this out and it will make God sit up and take note, "Bend an ear, God; answer me... Help your servant— I'm depending on you!" [Psalm 86:1 MSG].

QUESTION

In what way can you big-up God today?

_____

_____

BIBLE BONES

"We rely upon Jehovah our God" [2 Kings 18:22 Darby Translation].

God in disguise

"Who needs a doctor: the healthy or the sick? Go figure out what this Scripture means: 'I'm after mercy, not religion.' I'm here to invite outsiders, not coddle insiders"
(Matthew 9:12-13 MSG)

If it wasn't bad enough that Christian subcultures bubble out the world, I'm sad to say that they don't do much good for us either. *We aren't only bubbling everyone else out, we're bubbling ourselves in.* God isn't a big fan of either of the two realms we've manmade. He isn't exactly a faithful follower of the extremist uprising we've birthed. On one side we have the Christian culture, and on the other we have the secular side. We're meant to live in a happy medium, where there aren't any hitches or hurdles in our way.

QUESTION

Here's a tough one, where do you see yourself? Do you steer more towards the Christian culture or the secular side? Find that happy medium!

_____

_____

I hope I've got the message across loud and clear that bubbles trap us in our own wee world. It leaves us blind and deaf to the world's needs. Now don't take me the wrong way; I'm not saying its ok to date non-Christians, that's another subject I want to deal with another day. I'm just saying that we're living in two fanatical families instead of being one in Christ Jesus our Lord. Our identity is in Him, we've got to stop personalising our own translation of the Truth to suit ourselves.

Look at Jesus. He spent tons of time with the lowest of the low. He gave hard-hitting lectures on fake-faith rather than rebuking the lifestyles of those in desperate need. There's a breed of Christians who might as well be robots because they sure act like it! Their faith is built on formulas rather than forgiveness and good works rather than grace. It's as if they think that if they isolate themselves from the world and become a monk in a monastery they become the holiest of holies. This is topsy-turvy to the truth, God doesn't want His kids to start some sort of Christian-cult, He wants us to mix and mingle. To work in the world, to heal the hurts of the human race, but still be set apart from its secular sins. 1 Corinthians 1:1 (MSG) lays out the foundations of our faith, we are to be "believers cleaned up by Jesus and set apart for a God-filled life." **God singled you out, and set you apart so you would stand out for Him.** Never forget it.

QUESTION

What can we learn from looking at Jesus? Study His Word, turn to the New Testament and watch out for how He relates to "outsiders". Now, go and do likewise.

_____

_____

_____

_____

Take a minute to think about this strange truth. God is found where you least expect Him. He's found in the company of the crooked, the sin-sick, and those plagued with their past. If you shut out those who you don't think are up to scratch you are really slamming the door in God's face. You never know, they could be our very God in disguise, our masked Master.

Take a minute and think what is it that's so radical about Jesus? **He offers unconditional grace. He offers love to those who seek Him with reckless abandon.** So why have we made a tick-list of rules and regulations for Christianity? I believe if the Bible was to be written in one word it would be "grace". His load is light, so why do we lay back-breaking burdens on the broken and beaten? Last time I checked there weren't any conditions or eligibility criteria to becoming a child of God.

THINK UPON THESE THINGS

Beware. If you bubble-out "outsiders" you've pretty much snubbed off Jesus Himself. Imagine that. Read up on the story of the sheep and the goats, found in Matthew 25:31-46. Don't be caught out, catch yourself on!

living prayer

"When a believing person prays,
great things happen"
(James 5:16 NCV)

Never ever dare to dream of giving up on prayer. Prayer is perhaps the most priceless present God has given us. Prayer can transform even the most hopeless situations into a haven of happiness. Credit cards, lottery tickets and darling daddies are no competition to what God has to offer. Give it a try, give a prayer shout-out, after all, you have nothing to lose.

Here's a trial that God sent to test me a couple of years ago. The challenge was to see did I believe in prayer, I just about got the grade. Along with a couple of mates I went along to a summer mission, United Beach Missions, to share the Gospel with sightseers and seasiders. One of the biggest tests I came up against was not trying to teach the terrible toddlers but not giving up on a prayer that my friend, Rachel Creighton, dared to pray.

Our team was busy getting stuck in playing volleyball with the teens when a little girl with an upside-down smile came up to us and said that she had lost her ring that her granny had given to her, a prized possession. She was getting rather upset so my friend led a prayer as the three of us bowed our heads, asking God to help us find the ring. I was a bit cheesed off to be honest, because I figured that trying to find a ring in a beach is a bit like trying to find a needle in a haystack! And I'm ashamed to say that I reasoned we had more important things to do. But because I didn't want to disappoint the girl I kept searching, for what seemed like forever. When hope seemed hopeless we finally found it, I was about to give up that very minute.

Oh how we were relieved, the girl got back her ring back and I learnt a lesson. Prayer is not pointless, it's promising. And here's another thing, when you pray *expect to put in some time and effort to see things through.* That's a living-prayer, *acting out your belief.*

QUESTION	THINK UPON THESE THINGS
Write down some prayer requests. Now, what are you going to do about them? How are you going to put them into practice?	*Plea for prayer: never ever give in and give up praying!*
_____	
_____	
_____	
_____	
_____	

God-given gift

"It's in Christ that we find out who we are and what we are living for... he had his eye on us, had designs on us for glorious living, part of the overall purpose he is working out in everything and everyone"
(Ephesians 1:11-12 MSG)

Here's a word of advice, **whatever your gift is, embrace it**. *Cling to it*. Hold it as tight as you can and never let it go. Above everything else **don't let it grow old**. As it says in 1 Timothy 4:14-16 (MSG) "keep that dusted off and in use. Cultivate these things. Immerse yourself in them... Don't be diverted. Just keep at it." Don't you dare let yourself go rusty or else you might as well wave it bye-bye. God gave you your gift to work on it, not to snub it off and pay no heed to it. Don't keep it in the cupboard. When God asks you one day what you did with your gift, could you really hand it to Him covered in cobwebs and starved of sunlight?

Rick Hill spoke at our schools SU weekend-away, and one of the things he focused our heads and our hearts on was Colossians 3:17 (Amplified), "and whatever you do (no matter what it is) in word or deed, do everything in the name of the Lord Jesus". He said something rather special that's stuck with us since, **"use your whatever to worship."** Whatever your way to worship is God will take it. No matter how big or small your sacrificial service is, God will accept it with open arms. I'm telling you to try something new today. Worship God in a way you've never tried before. Finger-paint a picture, write a love-song or a love-letter, hand out free food or sweep the streets. Sing a new song and God will hear your worship loud and clear.

John 6 tells the tale of a young lad who didn't have much to give God. Before you go any further read John 6:1-12 to refresh your memory. Five small loaves and two teeny fish to be exact. A couple of crumbs could hardly fill five thousand hungry tummies, could it? Well, Jesus got to work, He got on His knees, praying He gave thanks for the food. God turned the little the lad had into a lot! Let that be an example to us all! **What will you give God?** A few measley morsels or a feast of thanks?

Here's another thing for you to chew on. You've got to foster and nurture your

QUESTION

What gifts has God given you? How can you put them into practice? Be specific!

_____

_____

_____

_____

_____

gift like a new-born baby until it grows to full maturity. It can't survive without you, so it looks like there's an awful lot of work to be done. God didn't say it was all going to be fun and games, but He did say that it would be rewarding. You have to be a good steward of your gifts, if you don't take it seriously you will have to answer to the Almighty one day.

POINT TO PONDER?

On Judgement Day could you have the cheek to hand your God-given gift over all listless and lifeless? It looks like there's some serious work to be done.

PRAYER

Father thank You for equipping me, I pray that I would put my God-given gifts to good use...

_____

_____

_____

a devil in disguise

"The love of money is the beginning of all kinds of
sin. Some people have turned from the faith
because of their love for money"
(1 Timothy 6:10 NLT)

(Before I begin I think I should say that having money is not a sin in itself!)

There's something that I have to get off my chest, call it a "religious rant"
or whatever you want. We owe God big-time right? Sure, He gave us His
most Priceless Treasure. So why do we try and short-change God? You know
exactly what I'm talking about, the offering plate is being passed around in
Church and you shove your hands into your pockets instead of into your
purse. Don't think you can pull the wool over God's eyes, you're going to have
to pay up one way or another so I suggest you square up now. You may not
be minted, you may not be mister or missus moneybags, but that doesn't
come into the equation.

Here's how it is, you need to dig deep down and find the guts to *give God
your all*. Luke 21:1-4 has something to say on us trying to rob God. The story
starts off with Jesus looking on as the rich put their gifts into the temples

treasury. What happened next is a rather important life-lesson for us all, Jesus "saw a poor widow put in two very small copper coins. "I tell you the truth," he said, "this poor widow has put in more than all the others. All these people gave their gifts out of their wealth; but she out of her poverty put in all she had to live on."" (Luke 21:2-4 NIV). If God doesn't have your all He doesn't have you at all, right? Do you know where I'm coming from on this one?

Here's the thing, *we're eternally indebted to God.* You could be a multimillionaire and give God big bucks and it still wouldn't be enough to pay off the debt. After all what price could you put on the death of Jesus, the Saviour of your soul? My Pastor, Mark McClurg, hit the nail on the head when he said "it may have been free but it wasn't cheap." It's so true, we owe God so why don't we show it. You know that your little goes a long way when you give it to God so why do you dig in your heels and stick to your stubbornness?

Some of you are probably thinking cash is cool but it can be quite the trickster, a devil in disguise. As 1 Timothy 6:10 (MSG) put it money is a bit like a ticking bomb, it can cause its captives to "self-destruct in no time." Looks like God knew what He was doing when He told us to hand over our pennies from our piggy banks, eh? It goes on to say that "Lust for money brings trouble and nothing but trouble. Going down that path, some lose their footing in the faith completely and live

> **QUESTION**
>
> *What are your reasons for being resistant? Write them down...*
>
> _____
>
> _____
>
> _____
>
> _____

to regret it bitterly ever after." **What's more important to you, your "fortune" or your faith?**

What's more important to you, your Master or your money? Being honest here, when was the last time you laid a sacrifice on the altar before God? Bearing in mind that a sacrifice has to cost you something, if it doesn't make much difference you can't call it a sacrifice. And while you're at it, don't give grudgingly.

PRAYER

You own all of me Lord, every penny in my possession is Yours for the taking. May I never chase after silver or gold, may I only ever chase after my God...

driving disaster

"You're not in the driver's seat; I am"
(Matthew 16:26 MSG)

My first driving lesson with my Dad didn't go as smoothly as I would have liked to say the least. I hopped into the car and set off up our lane. Everything was going hunky dory until Dad asked me to park beside his Merc. Now I'm not the quickest at getting my head around the ins and outs of how a car works. I didn't know what the clutch was for. No brownie points for guessing what happened next. I drove straight into the side of the Merc. Woops!

Pretty big blunder eh? And I hadn't even been in the car five minutes! That eventful episode not only left a dent in the car, but in my confidence too. It took quite a lot of guts to get back into the driving seat again, and quite a lot of time, a year and a half to be precise!

The moral of my story is not to panic and pack it in. My driving disaster reminds me of the way we get on with God. God has never ever given up on any of His children. He's stuck by our side every inch of the way. He's brought us through "thick and thin". And how do we repay Him? If we get in a muddle we screech to a halt and refuse to budge. That drives God mad. What God wants of us when we don't get it quite right the first time is to not let it put us off. *Learn from it* and **move on**.

Let's take a quick look at Joshua 1, it'll get your brain in gear for sure. God had given him a pretty major mission to accomplish. If I were in his shoes I think I would have skidded to a standstill, being blunt about it. God told

Joshua to lead His people into the land of Promise. Sounds like a rather sizable undertaking if you ask me! Here's what happened. God spoke to Joshua and told him that He would be with him just like He was with his ancestors, He promised He would never give up on him. Joshua 1:9 (MSG) puts it plainly, "God, your God, is with you every step you take". Don't ever question it, He isn't going anywhere!

You see, with God in the driving seat you will stay on track. With Him behind the wheel you can't go far wrong. That's what makes Joshua stand out from the crowd. He didn't try and grab God's steering wheel. It may not be smooth sailing, far from it, but that's no excuse to throw in the towel. I have had quite a few mess-ups since then, believe me, but **giving up doesn't get you anywhere.**

QUESTION

Why are we so quick to question? Why can't we just take Him at His word? Give a few thoughts...

_____

_____

_____

POINT TO PONDER?

Have you given up on God? Stick with it and God will stick by your side!

PRAYER

God, when I make a mess of it step in and do something great. Thanks for using me even when I feel fed up with myself. Thank You for never tiring of me...

_____

_____

a bog-standard bunch

"The Message that points to Christ on the Cross seems
like sheer silliness to those hellbent on destruction...
I'll turn conventional wisdom on its head, I'll
expose so-called experts as crackpots"
[1 Corinthians 1:18-19 MSG]

You may be wondering how did all those "super-saints" earn brownie points
from God? What did they have to do to get their picture framed and have
pride of place in the Hall of Fame? I used to think that they must have been
something "extra special". I thought that they were a rare breed that you had
to have been born into, and if you weren't, hard cheese. I lived under the lie
that ordinary folk, like you and me, just weren't good enough. I had convinced
myself that those "super-saints" were the smartest smarty-pants,
masterminds of their time, genuine geniuses.

But here's the truth, the apostles weren't brain boxes or boffins, they
were just bog-standard blokes. 1 Corinthians 1:20 [NIV] makes it clear why
God chose the outright ill-equipped, "Where is the wise man? Where is the
scholar? Where is the philosopher of this age? Has not God made foolish the
wisdom of the world?" There you go, God has chosen all the dunces to
dumfound all those clever-clogs who think they're know-it-alls. It's hard to get
your head round, isn't it?

So don't you fret pet, God can use absolutely anyone, including you! Talking
from experience here, I couldn't get my head around A Level biology, I knew I

was failing miserably. So I gave myself a hard time and beat myself up about it. I had somehow got it into my head that if I failed biology I had failed my Father. Something tells me that getting past those pearly gates is not determined by whether or not you pass biology. Thank goodness for that! (I got an E, you see). If you surrender yourself God will take you up on your offer, He won't turn you down.

God definitely doesn't just bring into play all the kids who are at the top of their game. You could be a high-school drop-out and God could use you just as much, if not more than a budding genius. It just depends on **how much you are willing to give up to God**. If you have a list of degrees and diplomas as long as your arm it won't get you a better seat in God's House, that's not the way it works! God isn't fussed on whether or not your trophy-cabinet is full to overflowing, or whether or not you have every certificate under the sun, because if you aren't under the Son, God can't employ you in His Kingdom-ministry.

POINT TO PONDER?

How much are you willing to give up to God? Be gutsy in giving! Spend some time telling God what you're willing to give. Write down your thoughts and your feelings. Always remember to be honest with yourself before you can be honest with God.

"pick'n'mix christians"

"You are my... portion"
(Psalm 142:5 NKJV)

I was wandering through Woolworths and passed the pick and mix stand one day when a random thought popped into my head- a fair few of us are "pick 'n' mix Christians". That got me thinking, these candy-Christians are more sour than they are sweet. They treat life like a pick n mix stand. They will have a little bit of this, and a little bit of that, but if they don't like the look of something they will steer well clear of it! It doesn't matter if they've never tried it before, they still snub it off. There's no persuading them; *they're so stuck in their ways they've left the Way and they aren't even aware of it.*

It seems to be becoming the latest trend at the minute, these candy-Christians think there's nothing wrong with taking a smidgen of prayer, with a rather large helping of worship, but sinking their teeth into the Bible or serving is out of the question. Sure, the super-size praise-portion makes up for it, doesn't it? That's hardly praiseworthy, is it? It may be hard to swallow but at least I say it like it is. There is definitely no sweet talking with me! God makes the menu; you can either take it or leave it.

So it looks like there's only one thing for it. You've got to take time to examine your life, spyglasses at the ready! Here's what I want you to do, weigh everything up and see if there's something lacking in your life. There's bound to be something that isn't weighing up right. A word of warning, you could be in for a shock, I was. My eyes were opened to the fact that I can be a bit of a "pick n mix Christian" at times. I can brush-off something I've actually never bothered to give a go, simply because I've never tried and tested it before.

After you've finished with your fine toothcomb here's the next step, you've got to change. It's not going to be easy, far from it. I've had to set time aside for studying the Bible, I felt like it was eating into my time at the start but now I've realised it's time well spent! I used to read my Bible every day but I was skimming instead of studying. If you aren't getting into the Word it's hardly going to get into your head, is it? And if it doesn't get into your head it can't sink into your heart!

If you aren't up for stepping up to the plate, before you know it, things

> **QUESTION**
>
> *Don't you dare read on until you've answered this question. Are you a "pick n mix Christian"? If so, what are you going to do differently?*
>
> _____
>
> _____
>
> _____
>
> _____
>
> _____

start to turn sour, and it rubs off on you; you become bitter. Sidestepping serving or bunking off Bible study turns you into a grumpy grouch. *You're missing out on God's blessings!* **All or nothing, that's what the Lord asks of**

us. Reading, praying and giving are all part of the deal, it may take some getting used to but it's well-worth putting the energy in. Here's another thing my eyes were opened to. God isn't fussed on fussy eaters; we've got to **feast at the Father's table**. I used to turn up my nose at the food that fuels my faith, not a smart move if you ask me. Ask God that He would give you a craving for Christ. *Taste and see that the Lord is good!*

BIBLE BONES

"Taste and see that the LORD is good" (Psalm 34:8 NIV) Go on, get your teeth stuck in to His Word!

a glimpse of God

"God's Word is an indispensable weapon"
[Ephesians 6:17 MSG]

Most parents give their babies building blocks or a bear to keep them out of mischief, well, my parents were a little different. To keep my brother, Sam, a happy chappy they gave him a Bible. It worked a treat! He went google-eyed at the sight of it, he would sit spellbound and pretend to read God's Word for goodness knows how long. But me, I was the complete opposite. If you gave me a Bible you might as well have put it through the shredder. I just ripped it up.

It goes without saying that I think much more highly of the Bible now than I did then. Here's one of my fav verses that makes me catch my breath every time I read it, it's found in 2 Timothy 3:16 [NIV] and definitely shouldn't be passed over, **"All Scripture is God-breathed"**. Let's just delve a little deeper, what that's saying is that God has breathed His life into the Sacred Scriptures, page after page is jam-packed with new life! Go on, take a lungful and *breathe in the beauty of our Lord!*

QUESTION

Has His Word found a home in your heart? I hope so!

_____

_____

But I've got to confess that there's something I've got to work on. I don't really realise how honoured I am to hold in my hands a book that's written by God Himself. The Bible is not just any old book, it's the Living Word. God took the time to birth a book and I make up lame excuses so as not to meet with Him. He sits on my shelf many a lonely day. Always remember that His Word has no power sitting on the shelf, we have to speak it out! Deep down I know that every time I pick it up to have a quick flick I stumble across God somewhere along the lines. He just jumps out at me! But still there I am, sitting on the sofa like a lazy lump instead of getting up and paying God a visit. Way to go Connie, way to go.

That having been said, here's what the Word of God is meant to be. Our *life-link* to our Lord, our lifesaver, we shouldn't be able to last long without it. I sincerely hope with all my heart that we can somehow get it into our thick skulls how *priceless*, how *precious*, this Book is. Its far more than a bunch of words scribbled down in a book, its Jesus! When I open the Bible all I can see is Jesus, a mirror-image, it's the spitting image of our Saviour. Take a look for yourself, you may just **catch a glimpse of God** if you look hard enough.

BIBLE BONES

"Every Scripture is God-breathed [given by His inspiration] and profitable for instruction, for reproof and conviction of sin, for correction of error and discipline in obedience, [and] for training in righteousness [in holy living, in conformity to God's will in thought, purpose, and action]" (2 Timothy 3:16 Amplified)

Don't just read it, worship... flick to an old favourite and read a chapter or two before you get down on your knees and thank God for His Word. If you're not sure where to start how about the gospel of John? Get to grips with God, get into His Word.

PRAYER

Father-God thank You for Your Word, a prized possession. May I meditate upon it day and night...

_____

_____

_____

modern day hermit

"Live in harmony with each other. Don't be too proud to enjoy the company of ordinary people"
(Romans 12:16 NLT)

Here's a challenge- leave the Christian bubble and enter the "secular world." We can't escape it, so why try and hide from it? I'm not saying to live like them but to live Jesus out in front of them. Romans 12:2 (Amplified) sums up what I'm trying to say, "**Do not be conformed** to this world [this age], [fashioned after and adapted to its external, superficial customs], but **be transformed** [changed] by the [entire] renewal of your mind [by its new ideals and its new attitude]." *Don't accept their culture, accept your calling.*

The frightening thing about Christian bubbles is that they invite us to withdraw from the world, to become a recluse, a modern-day hermit. We fear that the world will draw us in and we won't be able to escape from its snare. We act as if there isn't life outside of the Christian realm. Well, there is. You have to face the fact someday whether you like it or not. Here's the secret to success, *find the right balance.* It's kind of like God has gifted us with a spiritual set of scales and we've got to stay steady and not slip up.

One day I realised I wasn't as sure and steady as I thought so. There I was having a good wee chitchat on the phone to a friend, and we started chattering about all the Christian stuff we were involved in. When I got off the phone I was taken aback at how ashamed I felt when I thought about my stuffed schedule. My diary was so full of "God-stuff" there was little room left, I had everything boxed and bubbled. I bounced between prayer meetings, Bible studies, SU meetings and youth events. I could barely make the time to squeeze in "worldly" things with "worldly" friends.

> **QUESTION**
>
> *Have you got the right balance?*
> *Weigh things up...*
>
> _____
>
> _____
>
> _____

I can honestly say I couldn't remember the last time I met up with a few friends and just sat back and took time-out. Sometimes I feel like all I'm ever doing is spending my life in meetings rather than meeting needs. Take a word of advice from

> **QUESTION**
>
> *How about yourself? Do you stand in the same shoes?*
>
> _____
>
> _____

Romans 12:16 (Amplified), "do not be haughty (snobbish, high-minded, exclusive), but readily adjust yourself to [people, things] and give yourselves to humble tasks. Never overestimate yourself or be wise in your own conceits." I have to say I would prefer to close my eyes and ears to this verse because it makes my heart hurt when I sit down and study it. I see in myself that I've become so drawn into the Christian realm I'm withdrawing myself from my friends and family who aren't in the Church. I'm such a "christian" Christian, and I'm not proud of it! Learn from my slip-ups rather than from your own shortcomings. It would save you a lot of hassle and heart-ache.

Take a tick to listen to this hard-hitting message, "How then shall they call on Him in whom they have not believed? And how shall they believe in Him of whom they have not heard? And how shall they hear without a preacher?" (Romans 10:14 NKJV). It wouldn't kill us to meet up with our non-Christian mates at the cinema or hit the shops with the girls once in a while, would it? Acts 22:15 (MSG) was written for us just as much as for His followers back in Jesus days, **"You are to be a key witness to everyone you meet"**. How else are we going to reach them if we aren't getting in touch with them? It all boils down to this, how else are they going to meet Jesus?

POINT TO PONDER?

Are you ready to brave it and enter the "secular world"? Never forget that you're steady with Jesus by your side. Don't go it alone! Before you get up and go sit down and study Romans 10:1-17. Now, follow through on it.

geek for God!

"We're the Messiah's misfits"
(1 Corinthians 4:9 MSG)

I have a confession; I'm not the coolest kid. Far from it. Actually if I'm being really honest, I'm a bit of a geek. Yup, that's right. I was pretty much your average geek in junior high school I would say. I swotted away for hours on end and only gave myself a break every once in a while. I was the kid who was picked last for sport because I was a bit on the scrawny side, and I was the one who wandered the corridors alone from time to time, sad eh? I suppose I just never felt like I fitted in. I was a bit of a misfit, an odd ball, to tell you the truth.

Some of you are probably feeling sorry for me; I don't want a pity-party now you hear! And here's why, I mulled it over in my mind one day; is it such a bad thing? Should I change who I am? I came to the conclusion that I couldn't do a thing about it so I might as well accept who I am, born a geek always a geek I say! And that was the turning point. I made up my mind to be **a geek for God!** And do you know what, now I'm a geek going places for God, and you can jump on the bandwagon too if it takes your fancy!

I used to wish I could trade my life for that of my oh-so-cool brother and sister but now there's no way; I love being me! And here's why, when God works wonders in my life people stop and stare. They just can't get their head around how God works in this geeky girl. I would freak out inside every time my teacher asked me a question, but if someone turned around and asked me about God they couldn't shut me up!

I could imagine Joseph was a geek for God. He was a bit of a loner because he didn't get on much with his boisterous brothers. In my mind's eye I could see Joseph as being a skinny pasty-faced boy who was mollycoddled by his father. And I could see his brothers being rowdy and unruly strapping young lads, who took every opportunity to bully and badger Joseph. The whole hassle started in Genesis 37, when Joseph's brothers figured their father favoured Joseph more than all of them put together! Joseph's brothers plotted a bloodthirsty murder. Their plan was to put an end to Joseph's life and put an end to their fathers favouritism. Pretty extreme action if you ask me! What happened wasn't exactly what they set out to bring about. Joseph was sold into slavery simply because he wasn't one of the lads. And do you know where that got him, second in command of Egypt, pretty good going, eh?

I'm guessing some of you are thinking I've lost the plot, so I suppose I should put it plainly. Some folks think that geeks aren't with it, and maybe they're right, but here's where they're wrong- **God can use geeks**

> QUESTION
>
> *Can you think of any other geeks who were used to glorify God? Search the Scriptures for yourself...*
>
> _____
>
> _____

for His glory! Just think of John the Baptist, the loner Prophet who camped out in the wilderness; God spoke through him. Or Moses the middleman, he never fitted in anywhere; he was neither a prince nor a pauper. Yet God lead His people to the Promised Land with Moses as mentor. Or how about Noah, he was the laughing stock, the butt of all jokes. Everyone thought he was nothing more than a crazy clown, but God was able to *use this freak for His fame*. So there's only one thing for it, all you geeks get out there! Give yourself to God and just watch what He can do with a bunch of losers! *God can use your geekiness for His glory!*

THINK UPON THESE THINGS

Go on, be a geek for God!

chaos?

"Embrace peace—don't let
it get away!"
(Psalm 34:14 MSG)

Chaos. Love it. Why? Because in chaos we feel God's presence more than ever. We see God's hand working. We hear His voice. In total madness and mayhem our God reveals Himself to us. He is as real as our setbacks, bigger than our brain-bogglers and more powerful than our problems. When we feel powerless God is our strength. When we feel like we can't battle on any longer God fights for us. When we feel overwhelmed, broken and burdened, or at a dead-end God whispers to us that *He is our all in all*. All we need. Now and forever and always. One of the things I love-love about our God is that He "doesn't change—yesterday, today, tomorrow, he's always totally himself." (Hebrews 13:8 MSG). He is the Rock that we can cling onto in times of need, our steadfast Saviour, **"a very present help in trouble"** (Psalm 46:1 NKJV).

Elijah could teach us a thing or two about comfort amidst chaos. 1 Kings 19 is where you'll find the full story. The story line goes like this, Jezebel was plotting to do away with Elijah, so its no surprise that he upped and ran for his life! He even got so down in the dumps over the whole dilemma he cried out to God to strike him down. I could imagine him pretty-much praying for a lightening blot to strike him dead, couldn't you? But luckily for Elijah things definitely didn't turn out quite as expected, God created comfort out of the chaos. He never ceases to amaze me. Against all odds He always manages to find a happy ending to a sad story!

The story doesn't stop there. God told Elijah to go and stand on the mount so he could catch a glimpse of His glory. God paraded past, but He didn't show Himself in the wind or the quake. He didn't bring Himself into being in the flaming fire either- it was after the fire that God showed Himself in "a sound of gentle stillness and *a still, small voice*" (1 Kings 19:12 Amplified). Here's a wee secret about our God. He loves to do things a bit backward at times. What we would expect is no way near what we get! He has to teach us life-lessons that seem a bit cruel and uncaring at the time but it all works out in the end. Every time. God goes on to repeat His promise in Romans 8:28, memorise it, and then meditate upon it.

Here's where we're a bit backward. We think if we were to go on a quest to find God we would have to hike up a hill and meditate on an ancient mount. God isn't found on a holy hill. It's rather pointless going serenity-searching because it isn't like God is trying to make our lives a misery by playing hide and go seek. If you asked me where I thought God loves to hang out I would have to say in *the midst of chaos*, because that's where *a pocketful of peace* is. If you look past the pain you will always find God, in the heart of your heart. God places His peace inside each of us. If you just keep your eyes on Jesus peace will fill you to overflowing. Isaiah 26:3 (NKJV) pretty much sums up what I am trying to get at here, "You will keep him in perfect peace whose mind is stayed on You."

POINT TO PONDER?

When you're battling through bedlam, are your eyes fixed upward, or inward? Turn your eyes upon Jesus, that'll take your eyes off your troubles!

PRAYER

Father speak to me, still my heart. I thank You and praise You that You're my comfort in the midst of chaos. I'm praying for JOY independent of disasters...

_____

_____

_____

_____

jumble-sale junk

"Do not lay up for yourselves treasures on
earth, where moth and rust destroy and
where thieves break in and steal"
[Matthew 6:19 NKJV]

At the end of the day everything that we're stashing up for ourselves here on earth will come to nothing. Let's face it, it'll all fade away forever. Listen up, "don't hoard treasure down here where it gets eaten by moths and corroded by rust or—worse!—stolen by burglars. Stockpile treasure in heaven, where it's safe from moth and rust and burglars. It's obvious, isn't it? The place where your treasure is, is the place you will most want to be, and end up being" [Matthew 6:19-21 MSG]. **Set your heart on things above**, after all everything else will die off, "The earth turns gaunt and grey, the world silent and sad, sky and land lifeless, colourless" [Isaiah 24:4 MSG].

QUESTION

What have you set your heart on? Would it please your Father?

_____

Now hold on a sec, before you start blubbing your eyes out because all your bits and bobs will be no more, take a look at this. God has reserved a place for you in paradise, "an inheritance incorruptible and undefiled and that does not fade away" (1 Peter 1:4 NKJV). Seriously now, *what more could you want?* Just think about it, pretend God has had it with your pester-power and gave in to your pleas to allow you to cram your most priceless treasures into your coffin. You pack away to your hearts content, stuffing all your knickknacks into your casket, when you're finished you set off to your journey's end. When you get to Heaven you get busy unpacking your junk. Yip, you heard me right, your junk.

You see, everything you held dear on earth looks like jumble-sale junk when you get to Heaven. There's absolutely no comparison to be quite honest. Your "treasures" don't even come a close second when they are up against God's goodies. Just think about it- Jesus promised us that the best is yet to come, and He's hardly a promise-breaker! Heaven outshines it all, even our most sunshiny days will look dull and dreary compared to the glories of Heaven. The poshest palace is no match compared to our Heavenly Home.

I'm telling you, you've got to home in on this one- 1 Corinthians 2:9 (NKJV) "Eye has not seen, nor ear heard, nor have entered into the heart of man the things which God has prepared for those who love Him." Can't complain there can you? Here's another way of looking at it, it's like God's exchanging your bargain-basement belongings for top-notch trinkets, and swapping your third-class cabin for a first-rate room, no expense spared, and you're throwing a wobbly because it's out with the old and in with the new.

BIBLE BONES

"Get yourselves a bank that can't go bankrupt, a bank in heaven far from bankrobbers, safe from embezzlers, a bank you can bank on. It's obvious, isn't it? The place where your treasure is, is the place you will most want to be, and end up being" (Luke 12:33 MSG).

the story of Teddy Edward

"Now that we know what we have—Jesus, this great High Priest
with ready access to God—let's not let it slip through our
fingers... So let's walk right up to him and get what he is
so ready to give. Take the mercy, accept the help"
(Hebrews 4:16 MSG)

One day when I was a tiny tot I was playing with my teddy, Eddy, and disaster
struck! Teddy Edward's arm fell off! I can still remember to this day the sheer
panic I felt. I was so distressed by the whole ordeal that I quickly scampered
downstairs to find my mum, clutching my teddy in one hand and its arm in
the other. It felt like forever but I finally found my mum and pleaded with her
to patch-up my pal and make him all better. My mum said not to worry, she
would sort it out in a jiffy. Phew! I breathed a sigh of relief and ran upstairs
again... still holding the teddy! To this very day Teddy Edward has not been
fixed. I never gave him to her mother. Shame on me.

You have got to admit whether you want to or not, we treat God like this.
A lot! We bring our prayers to Him and set our worries down before His
throne, only to pick them up and carry them away again when we're done
with chanting our "prayers". This is not the way prayer works. This is quite
possibly one of my biggest struggles. I have such a burden on my heart for
Fermanagh. Ever since I moved house I fell in love with the people. Sometimes
I just can't seem to shake my prayer petitions off and leave my burdens with
the Lord.

In 1 Peter 5:7 [NKJV] it gets right to the heart of the matter, **"casting all your care upon Him**, for He cares for you."** Don't bring God your problems only to take them away with you again. We all know that every prayer matters and every prayer makes a difference, so why don't we cast our burdens before the Lord and leave it at that? Let go of your worries and let God work His wonders. Leave your prayers at the Throne of Grace. *Unburden yourself.* Let go and let God. Never forget that He wants your all, fears and failures are part of the parcel. If you hand over your problems to God He will hand over His peace. Sounds like a good deal, doesn't it?

BIBLE BONES

"You've carried those burdens long enough"
[Zephaniah 3:18 MSG]

PRAYER

Father, I have carried my cares for far too long. Here they are, once and for all, I'm laying them down before Your Throne and leaving it at that...

_____

_____

_____

walk your talk

"show the way for others"
[Matthew 5:19 MSG]

Guys and girls who don't walk their talk aren't "the real McCoy" to put it politely. Jesus didn't put it quite as politely, going as far as calling Pharisees frauds. Cutting to the chase He said "Your lives are roadblocks to God's kingdom" [Matthew 23:13 MSG]. We can be a barrier or a boulder in someone else's faith without even knowing it. Whichever one you are you're still a bother. If we dare to turn a stray sheep away we too are double-dealers. *If you turn your back on the lost you are turning your back on the Lord.*

Have a read at Matthew 23. It's pretty hard hearing mind you! Jesus got it out in the open. Here's what He said- "The religion scholars and Pharisees are competent teachers in God's Law. You won't go wrong in following their teachings on Moses" [Matthew 23:1 MSG]. That isn't all that bad now, is it? Sounds like Jesus stretched to giving the Pharisees a compliment rather than a criticism? Well, not exactly. Read on. He's about to change His tune. Here's what came next, "But be careful about following them. They talk a good line, but they don't live it. They don't take it into their hearts and live it out in their behaviour. It's all spit-and-polish veneer" [Matthew 23:2-3 MSG]. Ouch. That cut deep. So if we talk the talk but don't live the life we're no better than those snakes who slithered about, back in Jesus day.

Here's another point to ponder. If you're getting in the way of a kid coming to know the King, you'll get what you deserve. Here's what Jesus has to say about fake Pharisees, "Knowing the correct password—saying 'Master, Master,' for instance— isn't going to get you anywhere with me... I can see it now—at the Final Judgment thousands strutting up to me and saying, 'Master, we preached the Message, we bashed the demons, our God-sponsored projects had everyone talking.' And do you know what I am going to say? 'You missed the boat.' " [Matthew 7:21-23 MSG].

> QUESTION
>
> *Do you practice what you preach? Or does your walk foul your faith?*
>
> _____
>
> _____
>
> _____

It's like it was the last call to get on board and the religious scholars missed it a mile out because they were in their own wee world. *Don't be stuck standing in their shoes.*

Watch out. Nobody is immune to becoming infected with "hypocrititious", it slowly but surely kills you from the inside out. You see, the modern day religious rights movement is just as bad as back in the olden days. There is a list of do's and don'ts that rivals the Pharisees rulebook in the time of Jesus. Don't misunderstand me; there has got to be Christian standards. God never intended us to be sloppy Christians! But it looks like we've gone too far; our noble intentions of **trying to be "clean-living" has isolated us from the people who need to be shown love, not laws.**

POINT TO PONDER?

Do you have a list of laws rather than a life of love?

scatterbrains and scaredy-cats

"we possess this precious treasure [the divine
Light of the Gospel] in [frail, human] vessels of
earth, that the grandeur and exceeding
greatness of the power may be shown
to be from God and not from ourselves"
(2 Corinthians 4:7 Amplified)

Here's a quick question for you to think about. How can God possibly use
losers? Why is it that God seems to set apart the biggest scatterbrains and
scaredy-cats for something special? I ask myself this all the time. You would
think that He knows better than to take the trouble!

I see it like God's going to an orphanage to hand-pick His children. He
sweeps past the brightest and the best without a second glance, and heads
straight for the kid in the corner. *All the invisible children who everyone
closes their eyes and ears to God gathers into His arms.* That's how it works.

And here's why. God chooses the lowest of the low and the weakest of the weak so that *there never is any question about the source of power* that turns the world topsy-turvy for Jesus! **It has nothing to do with us, and everything to do with the power of God in us.** It's all about the power of the Message we live and preach day in and day out!

Just think of Peter at Pentecost. If I were you I'd have a sit-down and study the story. It's found in Acts 2. Here was a man who "tripped up" as often as he took a step, who always said stupid things, yet God used him in a mighty way. The day fire fell down, the disciples were filled to overflowing with the Holy Ghost. It was a spiritual mile-stone in the life of Peter, the day he realised he possessed a priceless treasure gifted by God Himself.

I'll never forget the first day I did a proper sermon. I was a teeny teenager, I wasn't big or brainy. I just knew Jesus and had to share Him. Now I want you to bear in mind that I was the painfully quiet kid in the class who whispered my one-word answers and took a complete beamer if anyone so much as spoke to me. The thought of standing up and speaking out scared me stiff. And yet there I was when the meeting wound up surrounded by a bunch of the cool kids from my school who never bothered with me before, telling me how awesome it all was. And they were right. God did an awesome work that day. You see, the thing is I'm just a cracked clay pot, a broken earthen vessel on my own, but I **let God have a free-reign in my life**, and that makes all the difference.

Isn't it a relief to know that God doesn't choose His children because of what we are but because **He can see the potential in us**? He can see what He can make from us even when others would write us off as waste. God purposefully picks out all the "Joe-Bloggs" of the world. He picks all the commoners who aren't welcome to all "the big fancy dos", and all the freaks who were never invited to the cool kids parties. This is why, God doesn't need superman or superwoman- they glory in themselves. God just needs someone He can put in their place, serving Him. God is glorified in the nobodies like no-one else!

POINT TO PONDER?

Are you scared of speaking up for Him? Stand in His strength and He'll empower you.

PRAYER

Lord God I can't thank You enough for hand-picking me for your purpose. From this day forward I'm willingly giving You a free reign to work in my life...

_____

_____

_____

_____

_____

wait on the Lord

"What's God going to say to my questions?
I'll wait to see what God says... If it seems
slow in coming, wait. It's on its way.
It will come right on time"
(Habbakuk 2:1, 3 MSG)

How on earth are we ever meant to know what's our calling? Seriously, how are we ever meant to know what's our personal purpose? You would think it would be way easier if God just told us straight out what in the world we are meant to do, wouldn't you? It sure would save a lot of confusion!

One of my biggest fears in life is making the wrong choice. My choice. More than anything else I don't want to go my way because I know that always ends in disaster! I need God's firm hand on my shoulder directing me every step of the way. Here's what happens if you let God take the lead in your life, "He will cause your thoughts to become agreeable to His will, and so shall your plans be established and succeed" (Proverbs 16:3 Amplified).

Don't worry. I've been in the same boat as you before. For what seemed like forever I was crying out to God begging Him to tell me what He wanted of me. The minute I sent away my application for Uni I knew something wasn't right. God said "no"; I wasn't meant to go just yet. So I hung back, expecting God to tap me on the shoulder and turn me round, telling me which road I was meant to go down. No such luck! God kept quiet. Not so much as a peep, or a peek at my personal plan.

It drove me mad. I didn't know which way to turn when all I was meant to do was wait. Yip, that's what I said. **Wait**. For as long as it takes you're meant to sit still until God gives the word. There's no point getting all worked up about it like I did. You don't have to worry one little bit. His answer will come in the nick of time. All you've got to do is **give God the go-ahead** to guide and pray His leading in your life.

Do you know what I find really reassuring? *God isn't in a hurry.* It isn't like God gets His skates on and rushes around like a mad thing. He ambles through life. "God strolling in the garden in the evening breeze" [Genesis 3:8 MSG] - pretty picturesque huh? God isn't one to be hassled. He takes His time and enjoys every second.

That's the way it should be. No rush, no fuss. Just waiting on the Lord. It will all be revealed in *His perfect time.* And not a moment sooner! The chances are that God will test your patience but stick it out; it's well worth the wait! Wise words from Habakkuk 2:3 [MSG], "The revelation awaits an appointed time... wait for it; it will certainly come." You just have to plod on, steady on, and it will all turn out fine and dandy.

THINK UPON THESE THINGS

Plod on, steady on!

PRAYER

Father I'm praying for patience, I want to wait for Your perfect time. Give me the strength to choose Your will over my own, I don't want my feet to falter, I don't want to take a wrong step ...

_____

_____

hide and seek

"Once the commitment is clear, you do
what you can, not what you can't"
(2 Corinthians 8:14 MSG)

Don't ignore your God-given gift. You're probably scratching your head right now, wondering what it is. Don't worry, God will make it clear as crystal. In His time. To help you well on your way to figuring out your gift take some time over these questions. What makes your heart come alive? What makes you have that feeling of complete wholeness that goes from the top of your head right down to the tips of your toes? What do you feel you would be lost without? It could be teaching Sunday school or playing piano. It could be anything!

Now we all know that God loves to give gifts. He has got to be the most generous Gift-Giver you will ever come across. But here's something you may never have given much thought, God loves a bit of drama. He likes a good old game of hide and seek! Where's the fun in God handing you over your gift when you could hunt it down for yourself and learn a little on the way?

If you still don't have a baldy clue what service God wants to employ you in don't stress, just wait until He tells you, on His terms and in His time. My patience did wear a little thin when I was searching for God's hidden gift. But I have to say if God gave me the chance to change the way it all worked out I wouldn't do anything different. It was kind of like going on a mysterious mission. When I finally figured out what God had graciously gifted me with it felt like I was well on my way to piecing my life together jigsaw puzzle piece by jigsaw puzzle piece.

Another helpful hint would be to get stuck in there! Get in the game, don't sit on the sidelines! If you're "child-friendly" and you're free to help out at the kidz club what in the world are you waiting for? Or if you're a bit of a whiz-kid why don't you see if your youth leader needs a helping hand working behind the scenes? Or if you could spare a few minutes why don't you pop into your youth club early and help set up? Or you could always take yourself and your trusty guitar off to the nursing home down the road and have a wee sing-song? There's only one way to find out, isn't there?

When I didn't know what God wanted of me I was so willing to give anything a go to get my hands on God's best for my life; I did all sorts. I pretty much did anything and everything that was thrown at me. Yeah sure I realised I wasn't cut out for a lot, and I mean a lot of things, but I also realised that I would never know my personal plan until I rolled up my sleeves and got stuck in there. **Go for it, find your gift from God!**

POINT TO PONDER?

What makes your heart come alive? What makes you feel full to overflowing inside?
Write away... now, what are you going to do about it?

PRAYER

Father-God help me on this hunt to find my gifts. Help me to foster them and bring them to fruitfulness...

what's your message

"Go everywhere and announce the Message of
God's good news to one and all"
[Mark 16:14 MSG]

Do you know how far we've distanced ourselves from the world? Do you know how bad its got? We believe that we don't need to breathe the name of Jesus. Do you know why? Because we let our clothes do the talking for us. Sounds strange? But when you think about it, it makes sense. I used to wear a "Christian" badge a few years ago but then I stopped wearing it, not because I was embarrassed of Jesus but because I was afraid of hiding behind it and not speaking for myself.

Along the same sort of lines, we think that if we wear a t-shirt with a Christian message we can stop at that. We've done enough. That's hardly the message we get across. The

> **QUESTION**
>
> *Do you know where I'm coming from on this one? Examine your life, can you see yourself distancing yourself from the world in any way? If so, what are you going to do about it? How are you going to make it right?*
>
> _____
>
> _____
>
> _____

message we're screaming through the silence is that we're a stuck-up bunch of snobs who won't associate with anyone who isn't a carbon copy of ourselves. *It's hardly the Message we bring.*

Just think of the "stereotypical Christian", armed with his big black Book, wearing a suit and a sad smile. He keeps his mouth shut simply because he thinks he's done his duty so he can stop at that. Yes, don't get me wrong, Jesus did ask us to carry the Message- we're meant to carry Him in our hearts! Technically Jesus didn't say that we have to write laws in a book and lug it about all day long. **He said to write love on our hearts and live it out.**

Likewise we let the books we read do the talking for us. I have absolutely no bother with walking down the street with a Bible tucked under my arm, but then one day it got me wondering. Is it because I think that's enough? I don't need to tell them about Jesus because my Bible has said enough already?

> **QUESTION**
>
> *How can you live out your love? Try and be as creative as you can...*
>
> _____
>
> _____
>
> _____

People can't read a book without first opening it, same as they can't read your mind. We have so much "spiritual stuff" stored up in our head we've got to share it; no-one will know about Jesus unless we tell them! We've got in such a state we think we don't need to talk about Jesus. In fact, we think we don't even need to talk. *What's really loud and clear is that we don't care much about this Message.*

POINT TO PONDER?

What's your message?

the art of 'clean living'

"Therefore let anyone who thinks he stands, take heed lest he fall"
[1 Corinthians 10:12 Amplified]

There's a giant sized problem with being brought up in a Christian environment. Being serious here, it's a monster matter that most people steer well clear of. But I think we need to study this subject seriously today.

Here's the problem, when I was a kid everyone thought of me as a perfect little angel. When I got my report from my nursery school teacher, it said that I had good ground morals and knew the difference between right and wrong. Pretty deep stuff for a tiny tot huh? You're probably puzzling over this one wondering what in the world is wrong with that? Well here's where I went way wrong, when I was growing up I never felt like God had to forgive me for all that much because I was "a good wee girl".

Here's a little about me as a youngster, I went to bed when I was told to without kicking up a fuss, and I tidied away my toys without grumping and grouching. I never stole cookies from the cookie jar and I never missed a day at Sunday school if I could help it. I was never cheeky to my teachers or skived school, and I didn't get involved with "the wrong crowd". So I never felt all that bad. Actually, being honest here, I felt like God owed me something. A pat on the back for all my hard work! Shame on me. Way worse, I bring shame on God's name when I get on like that. I'm thinking you're probably stuck in the same boat as me? *So often we think we're super-saints rather than sinners. You would think that our faith has more to do with the art of "clean-living" rather than Christ.*

Read 1 Samuel 15, stick with it! It may be a bit hard going but don't give up on it. It tells a story about how Samuel found that King Saul had went on ahead and sacrificed sheep when he knew it was a no-no. Samuel had a thing or two to say about that! He went on a rant about self-righteous Saul, who shamelessly stuck up for himself by saying that he did obey God when it was clear he was a rule-breaker.

QUESTION

Have you ever been there before? Have you ever felt as if you were such a saint instead of a sinner?

_____

_____

_____

_____

Saul made a show of himself, it looked like he was seeking to serve God on the outside but he was self-seeking on the inside. Never forget that God knows you inside-out. Here's what Samuel had to say, "Do you think all God wants are sacrifices— empty rituals just for show? He wants you to listen to

him! Plain listening is the thing, not staging a lavish religious production"
(1 Samuel 15:22-23 MSG).

Pray for an "unusual gift". That God would expose sin in your heart. **You can't disguise your sin from God so there isn't any point in putting on an act and trying to fool Him.** God won't applaud you for playing it up, He won't fall for it. You can't play pretend that you're perfect. God isn't one to turn a blind eye. Even if you only ever told one wee "white lie" it would still keep you from Heaven. You will still end up in the same place as the one who committed a life-time of sin and rebellion from God. Now that's "the wrong crowd", you don't want to end up there. Hell is not a very nice place to say the least. Consider the weight of your sin. **Don't take for granted God's gift of forgiveness.**

THINK UPON THESE THINGS

Take some much needed time-out and come clean with your Father-God about what's REALLY happening in your head. Fill the space with your thoughts...

God the gardener

"My Father is the One Who cares for the Vine"
(John 15:1 NLT)

For my 18th birthday a friend, Izze, bought me a love fern; oh how I loved Erne the fern! Unlucky for Ernie I soon discovered that I don't have green fingers; gardening is most definitely not my gift. Apparently you can over-nurture a plant- death by drowning, not nice. That was the terrible tragedy of Erne the fern.

Thank God the Gardener He knows how to care for us. He is our Creator King, "The LORD Almighty, who planted you" (Jeremiah 11:17 NIV UK). He gives you His Word, the most soul-satisfying sustenance to feed upon. He shelters you from the wind and protects you from any prowling predators. Even though He may give us a good weeding every once in a while He promises "I'll build them up, not tear them down; I'll plant them, not uproot them" (Jeremiah 24:4 MSG).

Last year I prayed what some people would believe to be a stupid prayer, "Lord, keep me in the place of pruning." Sometimes it feels like God's out to mow me down but I can't blame Him. I really do need to have a good pruning to keep me in order. Do you know what? I don't regret that prayer in the slightest, because God knows how much I can hack. Being serious though, if you ever feel led to pray that prayer I'm warning you you've got to be prepared to reap the consequences. Be careful what you pray for, you might get it!

Here's another wee thought that's been floating about in my head. **Everything He does is for your own good**. Quick flick to Romans 8:28, it's all for our good and His glory. It may be hard to hear but our branches need to be pruned "because they were deadwood, no longer connected by belief and commitment to the root... So don't get cocky and strut your branch. Be humbly mindful of the root that keeps you lithe and green" (Romans 11:19-20 MSG).

It may hurt at times but if God hacks away at our life it's because it helps us to grow and mature to produce fruit. Keep in mind through the tough times that "I am the Vine; you are the branches. Whoever lives in Me and I in him bears much fruit. However, apart from Me you can do nothing" (John 15:5 Amplified). You will wither away and die on your own but with God being as green-fingered as they get, you will blossom and bloom!

BIBLE BONES

"I am the Real Vine and my Father is the Farmer. He cuts off every branch of me that doesn't bear grapes. And every branch that is grape-bearing he prunes back so it will bear even more" (John 15:1 MSG)

juke-box Jesus?

"I know all about your... tantrums you throw against me... I'll show you who's boss"
(Isaiah 37:28 MSG)

Prayer is about so much more that God giving and you getting. By the way we get on you would think that God is "our personal juke-box". You're in charge of the charts. You press the buttons you want and God gives you whatever you wished for. You choose the tracks and God gets on the job at the click of your fingers. Right? Wrong! That's no way near how it works. God is not at your service. You aren't in control. God's the Boss; He's not to be bossed about. Don't you dare tell God what to do. Stop ordering Him about, it should be the other way around!

Matthew 6:7-8 (MSG) is dead right, "The world is full of so-called prayer warriors who are prayer-ignorant. They're full of formulas and programs and advice, peddling techniques for getting what you want from God. Don't fall for that nonsense. This is your Father you are dealing with, and He knows better than you what you need." *You may not get what you want, but God will give you what you really need.*

The point of prayer is "raising holy hands to God" (1 Timothy 2:8 MSG), not about standing with open-hands ready and waiting for what you want; God doesn't give in that easily. Don't be such a greedy guts! Be gutsy for God in prayer, not gutted if you don't get what you set out to get your hands on. It's like we're toddlers throwing a tantrum; if we don't get our own way, our parents don't give in. Prayer isn't about pleas of possessions, it's about pleasing our Parent.

QUESTION

What's the difference between a "want" and a "need"? Take a long look at your prayer life. Come clean and confess.

_____

_____

_____

So here's what I want you to do, **raise holy hands to Heaven**. Pray for forgiveness for all those selfish rather than selfless prayers. Come on, pour out your praises and let God in on how thankful you are that He forgives and forgets. And while you're at it pray for God's will instead of your own, *allow Him to take control*. Always remember that this life is not really your own in the first place. And last of all, but not least, **be plucky in prayer**. Call upon God to change the way you perceive prayer. Ask Him to give you a new perspective. Go on, get to it, spend some quality time with God.

THINK UPON THESE THINGS

Prayer-troopers are born the moment they send-up a heart-cry to the Father. The point of prayer isn't about getting your "pigging mitts" on whatever takes your fancy, its about pleasing your Papa-God.

treasured

"God will never walk away from
his people, never desert
his precious people."
[Psalm 94:14 MSG]

Here's something that's not only mind-boggling, it's mind-blowing. *God thinks about you.* You fill His head and His heart. Psalm 139 is proof that God can't get you off His mind. Here it is...

"O LORD, You have searched me and known *me*.
You know my sitting down and my rising up;
You understand my thought afar off.
You comprehend my path and my lying down,
And are acquainted with all my ways
For *there is* not a word on my tongue,
But behold, O LORD, You know it altogether.
You have hedged me behind and before,
And laid Your hand upon me.
Such knowledge is too wonderful for me;
It is high, I cannot *attain* it." [Psalm 139:1-6 NKJV]

Go on, write God a thank-you letter. Thank Him for holding you dearly, thank Him for thinking about you... Don't hold back...

Here's what I want us to focus our head and our hearts on today, **"How precious are your thoughts about me, O God. They cannot be numbered!"** [Psalm 139:17 NLT] If you are ever having a down-day just flick to Psalm 139 for a cheer-up, verse 18 [NLT] goes on to say that "I can't even count them; they outnumber the grains of sand!" So let's get this straight. God's thoughts are more than every speck of sand on every seashore, and more than every star in the sky!

Let me paint a picture here of how precious and priceless you are. God has set off on a treasure hunt. He has His heart set on a one-of-a-kind jewel that He just has to have. He has His eye on the prize and He won't stop at anything to get His hands on it! Now, when God gets to the end of the trail you would expect Him to dig up some buried treasure but He doesn't do anything of the sort. You see the prize isn't gems or jewels, it's you. You're the **"special treasure"** [Exodus 19:5 MSG] that God seeks and searches for.

Listen to this, "God has chosen you to be a people for his treasured possession, out of all the people who are on the face of the earth" [Deuteronomy 7:6 ESV]. Just think about that; you're God's trophy-treasure. If God had a trophy-cabinet you would be in it! And if it hasn't quite sunk in yet wait till you hear this- "Today God has reaffirmed that **you are dearly held treasure**" [Deuteronomy 26:18 MSG].

THINK UPON THESE THINGS

You're precious and priceless in the eyes of God.

genuine Jesus

"Then Jesus said to the crowds and to his disciples, "The teachers of religious law and the Pharisees are the official interpreters of the law of Moses. So practice and obey whatever they tell you, but don't follow their example. For they don't practice what they teach. They crush people with unbearable religious demands and never lift a finger to ease the burden" (Matthew 23:1-4 NLT)

Here's another thing I'm sure a whole pile of us got way wrong when we were kids, Jesus is not a mug. He's no pushover. Let me explain. Our Lord is Love, but we misuse and abuse this gracious gift like nothing ordinary. We think that because God is Grace we can get away with whatever we want. Wrong! Just take a look at Matthew 23 for instance, Jesus found fault with the

Pharisees and He refused to let it go. He didn't think twice about confronting them when they got up to no good. He went on a full-scale religious rant about how they didn't practice what they preached. And on top of that He gave them an earful for loading men with laws and not even giving them a helping hand.

Jesus definitely didn't let the fake Pharisees pull the wool over His eyes, "Everything they do is for show" [Matthew 23:5 NLT]. And He doesn't stop at that, "What sorrow awaits you teachers of religious law and you Pharisees. Hypocrites! For you are careful to tithe even the tiniest income from your herb gardens, *but you ignore the more important aspects of the law—justice, mercy, and faith*" [Matthew 23:23 NLT]. He hit the nail on the head, just because God is the giver of grace doesn't mean that He gives it out willy-nilly to those who don't practice their preaching.

And if the religious rabbis thought that was bad enough they had it coming! "What sorrow awaits you teachers of religious law and you Pharisees. Hypocrites! For you are like whitewashed tombs—beautiful on the outside but filled on the inside with dead people's bones and all sorts of impurity. Outwardly you look like righteous people, but inwardly your hearts are filled with hypocrisy and lawlessness" [Matthew 23:27 NLT]. Jesus didn't mince His words did He? Point proven, Jesus isn't a pushover, He's some gutsy guy!

I want you to catch sight of Genuine Jesus. Open your Bible at Matthew 21:12-17, it shares the story of Jesus storming into the temple and driving out all the merchants who thought they could walk all over God and buy and sell on His turf. Jesus wasn't found whimpering in the corner, He was found in the midst of mayhem, overturning tables and making a right scene! Here's what He had to say, "My house was designated a house of prayer; You have made it a hangout for thieves." [Matthew 21:14 MSG]. He said it straight, no frills or fancies to it.

POINT TO PONDER?

It's clear that Jesus could stand up for Himself, but the question is will you stand up for your Saviour? Or will you stand by?

PRAYER

Lord Jesus I pray that I wouldn't let an opportunity pass me by, help me to show people who You truly are, whenever and wherever I can...

Babel-builders

"God won't put up with rebels"
(Psalm 34:16 MSG)

At first glance the Tower of Babel doesn't seem so bad. They wanted to build something that could reach Heaven and touch God. Not so bad, right? Let's take a closer look at why it all went "pear-shaped". Here's what the Babel-builders said to themselves, "Come, let's build ourselves a city and a tower that reaches Heaven. Let's make ourselves famous so we won't be scattered here and there across the Earth" (Genesis 11:1-2, 4 MSG). Yikes, think they went haywire somewhere along the lines and forgot Who this life is all about. They were trying to make something of themselves by building Heaven on earth if you like.

God wasn't overly impressed with their efforts when He came down to survey their building project. He didn't pass it on the grounds that "this is only a first step. No telling what they'll come up with next—they'll stop at nothing!" (Genesis 11:6 MSG). So here's how God handled it, He made each and every one speak a different language so they couldn't understand a word of each other and had to part ways. "So the LORD scattered them from there over all the earth... That is why it was called Babel... because there the LORD confused the language of the whole world" [Genesis 11:8-9 NIV]. If God didn't do something about it and make it snappy they could have started on a space rocket to reach the Castle in the clouds!

But we shouldn't be too hasty in voicing our verdicts because *we're no better*, we're Babel-builders. We have it in our heads that we can make it on our own. In reality we couldn't last a single second on our own; God is our heartbeat. We think that if we try hard enough we can earn our train ticket to Heaven and be out of here without delay. On the contrary! It's a slippery slope we stand on when we let go of God's hand and try and find our own foothold. *We won't accomplish a thing if we try and manufacture God's work.* God makes the blueprints in His business,. Trying to take it over is rash and reckless. **Leave it to God; He can handle it on His own.**

POINT TO PONDER?

Are you a Babel-builder? Are you trying to get to Heaven on your own grounds? If you are, watch out, you won't get too far without running straight into a dead end street.
Turn to Genesis 11:1-9. Can you spot any similarities?
Are you guilty of being a Babel-builder?

PRAYER

Jesus I admit it, I'm a Babel-builder. I don't want to go it alone anymore, that won't get me anywhere. From now on I'm leaving it to You...

reality-check

"Get along with each other; don't be stuck-up. Make friends with nobodies; don't be the great somebody."
(Romans 12:16 MSG)

Maybe, just maybe we have created two breeds of Christians? Do you agree or disagree with me? I believe that we've created two extremes in the faith, who are both trying to make their own way through life, plodding along a dirt-track rather than the highway to Heaven. There are those who have been sucked into the worlds ways and tag along without a second thought. And there are those who would do anything to shake off sinners, going their own way rather than following the Way, they have it in their heads that they know best.

Luke 7:36-50 speaks of how Jesus got it spot on. Here's a word of advice, **follow His example and you won't go far wrong**. The story starts with one of the Pharisees inviting Jesus to be his guest at a dinner-party. The holier-than-thou host was astounded when along came a "sinner" who anointed Jesus feet with alabaster oil. You could just imagine the Pharisees whispering to one another and throwing her frowns. They were far from being happy chappies.

Here's what happened next. The Pharisee said to himself, "If this man were a prophet, he would know who is touching him and what kind of woman she is—that she is a sinner" [Luke 7:39 NIV]. Jesus put him straight, don't be a snob. He's talking to you too! Be sure that He won't let you get away with it. You can't be looking down your nose at anyone or slag "sinners" because it's just not on. Jesus has got to be the most down-to-earth man that you'll ever come across, so if I were you I would **walk in His ways**. Yes, He was radical in His faith but He didn't take an extreme side. Go and do likewise.

This isn't something that has died out over the years, it's just as much a setback now as it was when frauds and Pharisees roamed the earth. Take a look at your life, do you walk in one of these ways? Some of us have absolutely nothing to do with "worldly" people, here's a reality-check, get over yourself. While on the other hand we treat non-Christians like "evangelism projects" rather than friends. Our hidden agenda kills our "evangelism" endeavour and we are left wondering why?

Here's the secret to finding the balance, build real relationships with non-Christians. Learn to "Love from the centre of who you are; don't fake it" [Romans 12:9 MSG]. It may be a stretch, but make a friend out of someone who isn't a Christian. Home in on this, I didn't say make them your mission, I said make them a friend. You never know one day you may be lucky enough to *lead them to your Best Friend.*

POINT TO PONDER?

Are you an "extreme Christian" or a happy medium? Weigh up your ways and wise up!

superheroes are human

"For we do not preach ourselves, but Jesus Christ as Lord"
[2 Corinthians 4:5 NIV]

Ever since I was a wee girl I pictured the apostles in my mind's eye as squeaky-clean, picture-perfect people who had their faith down to an art. These flawless and faultless men wore white robes and holy halos. I was so sure that they were the untouchables, no matter how hard anyone tried no one could come close to their saintliness.

My scribbley crayon-colourings in Sunday school were never up to scratch. They never made these "mini-gods" look good enough. But then I had an eye-opener, they're just inventive-icons of our imagination, they don't exist. Now let me make myself clear on this one, I'm not saying that Peter and Paul and all the rest of them never walked this earth, they did. I'm just saying we've made them out to be make-believe characters in some sort of fairytale, true-enough?

Let's look at Peter, one of Jesus' closest companions, he must have been something special because he was in "the inner circle", right? Some of Jesus saintliness must have rubbed off on him somewhere along the way? Yea, Peter was a great guy, God did a awesome work in him and through him, but he wasn't free from faults. Luke 22:31-34,54-62 tells a sad story, Peter denied and disowned Jesus. The story goes like this, Jesus was basically being dragged to His death and Peter followed from a distance.

Then there were some servants sitting around a campfire so Peter decided to hang about and see what was happening, waiting for a word. A servant girl piped up, "This man was with him" (Luke 22:56 NIV). His response, "Woman, I don't know him" (Luke 22:57 NIV). Far from the truth, eh? "A little later someone else saw him and said, "You also are one of them... "Man, I am not!" Peter replied.... About an hour later another asserted, "Certainly this fellow was with him, for he is a Galilean." " (Luke 22:58-59 NIV). Peter lost it. "Man, I don't know what you're talking about!" (Luke 22:60 NIV). As he was speaking, the cock crowed.

Let's take a look at Acts 10:26 (NKJV) , when Cornelius met Peter he fell at his feet and worshipped him like a god, here's what Peter had to say about that, "Stand up; I myself am also a man." We've raised the apostles on pedestals, they represent an exalted degree of spirituality that we don't have a hope of reaching? Right? Wrong, here's the truth, *they were just a bunch of common men, not supernatural saints! We* shouldn't forget who they really are. **"Superheroes" are human**. Now let's think about this, if they're no different from us, just as Peter said, what's stopping us? What are you waiting for, **go and do your bit!**

POINT TO PONDER?

What's stopping you from stepping up?

the Lamb of God

"The blood of Christ saved you. This blood is
of great worth and no amount of money
can buy it. Christ was given as a lamb
without sin and without spot"
(1 Peter 1:18-19 NLT)

Am I the only one in the world who thinks that Jesus doesn't exactly fit the frame of the man you imagined? "The servant grew up before God—a scrawny seedling" (Isaiah 53:2 MSG). Jesus wasn't as pretty as a picture and He wasn't built like a Greek god. "He was looked down on and passed over... One look at him and people turned away. We looked down on him, thought he was scum" (Isaiah 53:2-3 MSG).

Our King was sneered and jeered at, believed to have been a blasphemer, a stirrer of strife, a transgressor against God Himself. "We thought he brought it on himself, that God was punishing him for his own failures" (Isaiah 53:4 MSG). Deserved of a damning death, a dead-dog had more dignity. Strange, not the King you would expect? But I'm sure you will agree you wouldn't change a thing about Him!

There's a modern-day myth going about these days. Some of us have got it into our heads that Jesus was a bit of a pansy. No. He most certainly was not! How do I know that? No pansy would take our punishment. Turn to Isaiah 53 with me, and jut think about it...

"He was beaten, he was tortured,
but he didn't say a word.
Like a lamb taken to be slaughtered
and like a sheep being sheared,
he took it all in silence.
Justice miscarried, and he was led off—
and did anyone really know what was happening?
He died without a thought for His own welfare,
beaten bloody for the sins of my people.
They buried him with the wicked,
threw him in a grave with a rich man,
Even though he'd never hurt a soul
or said one word that wasn't true" (Isaiah 53:7-9 MSG).

See how He suffered? For you. Why don't you take some time out this very minute to thank Him for it. Take all the time you need.

Just think... **it was our sins that nailed Him to the tree and tore His heart to shreds**. "He took the punishment, and that made us whole. Through his bruises we get healed" (Isaiah 53:5 MSG). We're the deservers of death. "We're all like sheep who've wandered off and gotten lost. We've all done our own thing, gone our own way" (Isaiah 53:6 MSG). We left our Lord, we forsook our Father. Yet He brings us back. Punishment has to be paid. The

Lamb of God stepped up to the alter and took our place, our penalty and our pain. "God has piled all our sins, everything we've done wrong, on him, on him" (Isaiah 53:6 MSG). Not the King you would dream up, but everything you hoped for and more.

POINT TO PONDER?

Thank-God for His merciful grace! Thank-God for Jesus!

The ABC of becoming a Christian...

A each and every one of us has sinned, ADMIT it. Be honest with yourself, God doesn't accept excuses. Acknowledge your shortcomings, "all have sinned and fall short of the glory of God" (Romans 3:23 NIV). Ask God for His forgiveness and say sorry for your sins. Own up to the fact that your sins sent Jesus to the cross.

B you've got to BELIEVE that Jesus died to bring you new life. Jesus sacrificed Himself, He went willingly to the cross to take your punishment. God sent His Son to pay our penalty, "The payment for sin is death. But God gives us the free gift of life forever in Christ Jesus our Lord" (Romans 6:23 NCV). Jesus' sacrifice bought your salvation.

C it's time to CHANGE your ways, "anyone who belongs to Christ has become a new person. The old is gone; a new life has begun!" (2 Corinthians 5:17 NLT). Repentance, in other words, means living a changed life. If you say you love Jesus you'd better live like it! Make a change, live your life wholly for Him.